S† LO

ACR 9019

54 Yu, Su-mei.

Asian grilling.

11/02

DATE		

Asian Grilling

Also by Su-Mei Yu

Cracking the Coconut

Asian Grilling

85 Satay, Kebabs,

Skewers and Other

Asian-Inspired Recipes

for Your Barbecue

Su-Mei Yu

WILLIAM MORROW

An Imprint of HarperCollins*Publishers*

HarperCollins books may be purchased for educational, business, or sales promotional use. For information please write: Special Markets Department, HarperCollins Publishers Inc., 10 East 53rd Street, New York, NY 10022.

FIRST EDITION

Printed on acid-free paper

Designed by Ralph Fowler

Photographs by Richard Jung
Food styling by Rori Trovato
Prop styling by Robyn Glaser

Library of Congress Cataloging-in-Publication Data

Yu, Su-Mei.
    Asian grilling : 85 satay, kebabs, skewers and other Asian-inspired recipes for your barbecue / Su-Mei Yu.
       p. cm.
    ISBN 0-06-621119-0
    1. Barbecue cookery. 2. Cookery, Asian. I. Title.

TX840.B3 Y8 2002
641.5'784—dc21

2001054387

02 03 04 05 06 / IM 10 9 8 7 6 5 4 3 2 1

To Angela, you are my light

In memory of Italo Scanga,
Al mio amato Italo

Contents

Acknowledgments

An ordinary barbecue becomes a festive occasion when many pairs of loving hands are there to help and pitch in. So is the making of a book, especially a cookbook on grilling.

Harriet Bell, my editor at William Morrow/HarperCollins, sparked the idea for this book. Sarah Jane Freymann, my literary agent, helped fuel the fire. Weber-Stephens Products Group bestowed on me a gift of a Weber grill for recipe testing. And I could not have attempted to become the Asian Smoke Queen without my comrade-in-arms, Elizabeth Perini, my assistant, and my friend Lois Stanton. They chopped, minced, marinated, and skewered, testing every recipe, day after day, for months. Nikki Symington stood by ready to read and reread the entire book. The artistic team of Richard Jung, Rori Trovato, and Robyn Glaser not only captured the essence of *Asian Grilling* but turned the food into mouthwatering works of art. My companion, Italo Scanga, and his studio crew, as well as friends Lucy Goldman and Evonne Schulze, tasted and critiqued the recipes. It was a job they relished and undertook with gusto. It's been one memorable party.

Introduction

WHILE VISITING my sister, Marian, at her home
in Lampoon (a small town outside of Chiang Mai, in
Thailand) early one morning, I set out on my daily
walk along the rice fields. I came upon a group of villagers standing
underneath a shady tamarind tree, watching as several men with a
giant water pump sucked the water from the irrigation canal that
encircled the vast rice fields.

Throughout the day, I heard the engine humming from Marian's
home. By late afternoon, when I walked back to the canal, the villagers were still there, sitting and watching. After a while, the ancient
and exhausted pump engine finally gave out.

Dressed only in skimpy loincloths, the workmen clambered down
to the bottom of the canal, which was now mostly mud, to capture
the remaining fish, frogs, and other living creatures with bamboo
fish traps. They transferred their catch from the fish traps to plastic
buckets. As the sun began to set, women arrived with buckets of
water. While the men washed and changed into dry clothes, the
women made numerous trips to nearby wooden huts. They returned
with a crock of fermented fish paste and baskets of greens, chiles,
and limes. A young girl brought bamboo baskets filled with warm
cooked sticky rice. Someone else added a chopping board, knife,

and large terra-cotta mortar with a wooden pestle to the growing collection.

The men gathered kindling and dry leaves for a fire. They chopped down young bamboo branches from a nearby grove, which they whittled into long thin sticks. After starting a fire, they turned their attention to the crayfish, crabs, frogs, and assorted large and tiny fish. Scooping the wiggling creatures from the plastic buckets, the men proceeded to skewer the live fish and frogs on the bamboo sticks, pat each stick with salt and pepper, and prop it carefully over the crackling fire to cook.

Meanwhile, one of the women dropped handfuls of crayfish and crabs into the mortar, pounding them with garlic, chiles, salt, fermented fish paste, and lime. As the food cooked, everyone relaxed around the fire. An old man pulled a bamboo flute from his sash and started to play. I was invited to sit by the fire and share the meal.

Waiting for the fish and frog skewers to grill, everyone drank homemade moonshine and ate fiery, spicy crayfish and crab salad complemented by the warm, chewy sticky rice. By the time the last fish had been eaten and the moonshine drained to the last drop, the moon had risen high in the sky, and it was time to go home and go to bed.

I remember my enjoyable adventure in Lampoon as a tiny snapshot, revealing how life must have been in Thailand and throughout the rest of the world when food was hunted, foraged, and cooked over an open flame. Even with all of our modern conveniences, nothing tastes as good as food cooked outdoors.

Nowadays, our path has taken most of us far from the forest and fields. Hunting and gathering has faded into the mists of another time. But we happily continue to cook outdoors, enjoying the benefits of this very primitive, ancient cooking method. In doing so, for a moment we capture a sense of timelessness and the cycles of our lives.

Grilling remains a popular and traditional way of cooking throughout Asia. The cooks of Thailand, Laos, Cambodia, Myanmar, and Vietnam all employ similar grilling methods, revealing a shared history of cultural connections and exchanges. In other parts of Asia, particularly China and India, renowned for centuries of culinary arts, grilling techniques came from the Mongols, masters of grilling, who once occupied both countries.

The Japanese, preferring the austere and minimal, grill food with simplicity and clean taste. Korean grilled food, on the other hand, exalts the country's love for sweet flavors. Indonesians created the famous satay, tiny skewers of food grilled and dipped in savory sauces.

Today, grilling retains its universal appeal. Once, in many Asian countries, kitchens were separated from the main house, and often outdoors. Grilling was not only a practical way to cook, using the natural fuel sources, but also a sensible way to conserve fuel. Today, modern homes with built-in kitchens have replaced the outdoor cooking pit and fire, but Asians continue to grill, building small fires in self-contained pits on dirt floors somewhere in their yards. Modern portable grills of all sizes are also available and popular in many Asian homes.

If you enjoy cooking outdoors, grilling with an Asian accent will add a new sense of adventure and flair to your culinary repertoire.

In the beginning was the fire. Then came the grill. The unique flavors and tastes of the Asian grill await you.

Equipment

Cooking directly over an open fire remains a popular technique throughout Asia. In Southeast Asia, where metal has always been a scarce commodity, grills are often simple, homemade contraptions constructed from recycled materials. Small grills are rectangular metal boxes made from tin, while larger ones are constructed from used metal drums. Racks are fashioned from heavy-gauge chicken wire. The Japanese favor the hibachi, a small tabletop grill, for indoor and outdoor use. In India and Korea, a large earthenware jar is used for grilling and smoking.

Here there are many types of grills to choose from that use gas or charcoal as the source of fuel. They range in size from portable tabletop models to enormous high-end grills with all sorts of bells and whistles. Each one has its pros and cons. Gas grills are quick to ignite, with relatively little cleanup. (Note that now there are even models that use a gas igniter to start a charcoal fire.) A fire made with charcoal briquettes or lump hardwood charcoal is much hotter and lends that true grilled flavor to food. I own two grills, one gas and the other a Weber kettle grill. All of the recipes in this book were tested on both.

You will also need bamboo and flat metal skewers for satay, kebabs, and other recipes. Get yourself an inexpensive chimney for lighting the grill, if not using a gas grill. Spring-loaded long-handled tongs and a long-handled spatula are essential for turning and lifting food. Good thick oven mittens will make it easier to turn food over an open fire. You'll also need them to turn the chimney over and dump out the coals. A fine-mesh metal rack that can be placed on top of the main grate is a must for cooking vegetables, fruits, shrimp, some fish, and flatbread. A handheld fan is handy for rousing a dying flame, and a spray water bottle puts out shooting flames.

Keep in mind that cooked food, especially meat or seafood, should never be placed on a platter that held uncooked food. Keep an extra plate or disposable pan at hand. After the food is cooked, while the grate is still hot, you'll want to use a stiff wire brush to remove any residue.

How to Build a Charcoal Fire

Food cooked over charcoal tastes better than food cooked over gas. The more intense heat sears the food, browning the outside layer. Once the flames die down, the ash-covered red embers provide constant heat that allows food to cook evenly. When the embers have burned down even further, the heat will be just right for cooking flatbreads. Finally, the hot gray ashes are just the right temperature for cooking sweet potatoes and taros.

Although charcoal briquettes are readily available, I urge you to search out lump hardwood charcoal, which is pure charcoal and burns evenly. It is also closest to what Asians use to fuel their grills. Charcoal briquettes are convenient, but they contain additives that impart a chemical taste to grilled food.

Using a chimney is the easiest and most efficient way to start a charcoal fire. Stuff a couple of pieces of newspaper into the chimney's bottom and fill the top of the cylinder with charcoal. Set it in the grill. Light the newspaper with a match through the holes in the bottom of the chimney. The flames will move up, igniting the coals; once they are red hot (10 to 15 minutes), use a heavy mitt to turn the chimney over, and dump out the coals. Add more charcoal if necessary; the hot coals will ignite the newer coals. For most cooking, you want the coals to be hot embers covered with a coating of ashes, which will take 30 to 45 minutes, depending on how much charcoal you add to the grill. Another test for readiness is to place your hand 9 to 10 inches above the coals, and count slowly: "One Asian grill, two Asian grills . . ." If you can keep your hand over the coals for a count of "three Asian grills," the heat is high; six counts means medium; and nine means low.

High heat is used in Asian grilling to sear meats quickly and to grill eggplants and peppers. Placing the food close to the high heat causes the outside to char, while the interior becomes soft and tender.

Foods wrapped in banana, pandanus, or bamboo leaves or aluminum foil should be grilled over medium heat. The wrapping keeps the surface of the food from scorching. Meat, poultry, seafood, and vegetables cooked in this way remain moist and soft, and, if wrapped in leaves, absorb the plants' perfumes. Satay of thinly sliced meat and kebabs should be grilled over a medium-high heat.

Large pieces of meat and whole chickens, fish, and shellfish are best cooked over medium-low heat by what's called the "indirect" method. With a garden trowel, rake the burning coals to one side of the grill. (I like to add dried herbs or coconut to the coals; chunks of fruitwood work well, too.) Replace the grate, place the food over the area without coals, cover (be sure to open the holes in the cover), and slowly grill-smoke. The results are similar to those from an Indian tandoori oven: moist, tender food with a smoky flavor.

Asian Flavors

Asian foods are often seasoned with nothing more than a sprinkling of salt and pepper, a squeeze of lime, or a dash of vinegar. Marinades are used as seasonings and to tenderize tough cuts of meat and game. Daikon, coconut cream, fresh pineapple, papaya, and ginger are frequently used to marinate food.

Each region, however, has its own distinct flavors for grilled food. In Southeast Asia, salt, garlic, lemongrass, galangal, fresh turmeric, and white peppercorns are signature ingredients. Sesame oil, soy sauce, cinnamon, five-spice powder, and ginger flavor Chinese food. Dried spices such as chiles, nutmeg, mace, cumin, cinnamon, and black pepper predominate in Indian cooking. Koreans prefer sesame oil, sugar, soy sauce, and scallions. In Japan, soy sauce, miso, mirin, bonito flakes, and sugar are used. Ginger, shallots, turmeric powder, coriander seeds, and cumin spice up the cuisines of Indonesia.

Throughout Asia, fresh and dried ingredients are pounded, ground, or pureed into pastes that are used as marinades. Although you can use a blender, I'm an advocate of traditional cooking techniques and prefer the mortar and pestle.

Select a mortar with an inner diameter that measures at least six inches. I use a Thai granite mortar and pestle—these are available in large Asian markets. Place the mortar on a sturdy waist-high work surface, and slip a dish towel under it to keep it from sliding. To grind dried and dry-roasted spices and nuts, hold the pestle like a cooking spoon. With one hand cradling the mortar, press the pestle against the center and sides of the mortar in a circular motion. To puree wet ingredients, hold the top of the pestle like a walking stick, and strike it straight up and down into the center of the mortar. As the ingredients creep up the sides, use a spoon to push them back down.

If using a blender, the results will not look or taste like marinades made in a mortar and pestle. Dry-roasted dried herbs and spices must be ground separately before they are added to the blender with other ingredients. Fresh ingredients such as mint and ginger must be finely chopped or minced before adding them to the blender, to ensure a smooth texture. You will also need to add a tablespoon or so of vegetable oil to the blender.

Finally, the most important thing to remember when grilling is organization and efficiency. Have everything ready and within easy reach before you begin cooking. Most of these recipes, once the food is marinated and the dipping sauces prepared, take very little time.

Once the fire is ready, it is essential that you start cooking. The key to perfect grilling is keeping a constant watch over the cooking process. This need not be a lonely vigil. Like the preparation, grilling can be a shared experience, with friends and family pitching in to help.

There is something exhilarating and liberating about cooking outdoors, especially when you can experiment with new flavors and tastes. Food seems to taste better in open air. The smell of the fire and the aromas of outdoor cooking beckon and welcome others to your table or picnic blanket. Let's share in the delights of the fresh air, fresh tastes, and friendly art of Asian grilling.

Satay, Kebabs, and Skewers

I WAS BORN and grew up in Bangkok, Thailand, in a neighborhood crammed with rows and rows of identical shophouses. Each shophouse had two rooms, one at street level, where people had their businesses, and one upstairs, where they lived and slept. These tiny houses were packed together like matches in a box and faced one another across narrow, crowded alleys.

Every day, from the crack of dawn until late evening, waves of street vendors selling snacks, vegetables, fruits, meat, and live chickens, along with people who repaired everything imaginable from broken ceramic bowls to leaky metal pots, passed through the neighborhood.

The satay man, one of my family's favorite vendors, came through once or twice a week, always late in the afternoon. Balancing a portable charcoal grill on one end of his bamboo pole, he carried a cabinet filled with uncooked skewers of marinated pork, a pot of peanut sauce, and some cucumber relish on the other. My parents were very strict about not allowing us to eat snacks between meals, but when the satay man sang, "Satay—a—a—a," even Mama gave into temptation.

The irresistible, mouthwatering aroma of sizzling meat on the satay man's grill was impossible to ignore. "Oh, just a plate or two, not so much as to spoil our appetite," Mama would say as she signaled him to stop right at our very doorstep. But we never stopped at a plate or two. Once we started eating those crispy, juicy pork satay, dipped into the rich, creamy peanut sauce and accompanied by the sweet-sour-spicy cucumber relish, we ate until we were stuffed.

Years later, when I was introduced to American-style grilling, it made me homesick for the satay man's food. My husband, like any American man, loved to barbecue. Indoors or out, it didn't matter. He loved his tiny hibachi grill, and often cooked one of his specialties, curried chicken livers wrapped in bacon, right on the dining room table. For outdoor cooking, he splurged and bought an expensive Korean ceramic grill that turned even a humble hamburger into a gourmet dish.

When it comes to grilling, satay, kebabs, and other skewers are my favorite dishes. They are nothing more than morsels of meat, poultry, seafood, or vegetables threaded onto wood or metal skewers and grilled over a hot fire.

Satay are small thinly sliced pieces of marinated meat, poultry, or seafood tightly laced onto thin bamboo skewers. Placed close together over a hot fire, a handful of skewers can be flipped over with tongs at the same time for even cooking, and to prevent burning. The marinade is brushed on the meat during grilling to keep it moist. Satay cook in a matter of minutes, and are eaten while hot.

Kebabs are made with larger pieces of meat, chicken, game, seafood, or vegetables, threaded onto metal or wooden skewers. Sometimes paper-thin slices of meat or chicken are laced onto skewers and pressed tightly together, so they resemble one solid piece of meat. If kebab ingredients are not marinated, a simple sauce is brushed on during grilling. Kebabs are placed on the grill close to one another, but not as close as satay. They are usually served as a main course.

For skewers, a longer metal or wood skewer, or even an aromatic stem of lemongrass or sugarcane, can be used to pierce a whole fish, chicken, or shrimp. A common method of grilling this way in Asia is to suspend the loaded skewers on a hook over the fire, as for char siew, or barbecued pork from China, or tandoori from India. Thailand, Laos, Cambodia, Vietnam, and Myanmar use similar methods with their own variations.

To grill satay or kebabs, it is important to know the types of skewers and how to use them.

Natural skewers, such as wooden sticks, split bamboo, and aromatic branches such as lemongrass stalks   Thin branches are best for small pieces of meat, poultry, seafood, and vegetables. Larger sticks are used for whole chicken, duck, or fish. To prevent wooden or bamboo sticks from burning, soak them in cool water for 30 minutes, then drain and dry before using. Aromatic branches do not require soaking.

Metal skewers   Short or long, thin or thick stainless steel skewers are available in hardware stores, cookware shops, and supermarkets. I use the shorter versions (12 inches) for individual servings and longer ones (16 inches) for larger pieces or whole chickens. Most are ⅛ to ¼ inch wide. For solid pieces of meat, poultry, seafood and vegetables, thin flat blades are best. For meatballs, use square-shaped skewers so the food won't slip. Oil the skewers lightly with vegetable oil before using to keep the food from sticking to them.

Nonya-Style Chicken or Pork Satay

WHEN HE WAS YOUNG, my father traveled throughout Southeast Asia as a salesman. I loved to hear his tales of adventure and food, such as his descriptions of satay vendors in Malaysia and Singapore. Papa said that each vendor had three or four metal grills going at the same time. The vendor would stand in front of the hot grills, engulfed in smoke, flipping, turning, and basting the tiny skewers all at the same time. As he slapped a handful of cooked satay onto a plate, a line of eager customers quickly snatched up the prizes and plunged the cooked skewers into bowls filled with different types of sauce. The price of a meal was based on the number of sticks picked clean.

Nonya cooking is a fusion of Malaysian, Indian, and Chinese cooking. The marinade ingredients for chicken and pork satay have slight variations. For chicken, the cumin is left out; the marinade for pork satay has no turmeric. Pork is not eaten by Muslim Malaysians, but it is the favorite meat of the Chinese. Serve the satay with Indonesian Peanut Sauce (page 141) and Indonesian-Style Cucumber Relish (page 152).

Marinade

Makes 2⅓ cups

1 teaspoon coriander seeds
1 teaspoon cumin seeds (for pork satay)
½ teaspoon sea salt
4 fresh bird chiles or 2 red serrano chiles, minced (1 tablespoon)
1 stalk lemongrass, tough outer layers and green parts removed, minced (¼ cup)
1 teaspoon turmeric powder (for chicken satay)
3 shallots, minced (⅓ cup)
1 tablespoon ground blanched almonds
1 teaspoon red miso
½ cup combined coconut cream and milk (the consistency of whole milk) (see page 135)

Make the Marinade

1. Put the coriander seeds in a small skillet and dry-roast over medium-high heat, sliding the skillet back and forth over the burner to prevent burning, until the spice exudes a pleasant aroma, about 1 minute. Remove from the heat and transfer to a bowl to cool. Repeat with the cumin seeds, if using. Grind in a spice grinder and set aside.

2. Pound the salt and chiles in a mortar with a pestle into a paste. One at a time, add the lemongrass, coriander (and cumin) seeds, turmeric powder, if using, shallots, almonds, and miso, in sequence, adding each one only after the previous ingredient is pureed and incorporated into the paste. Transfer to a mixing bowl and add the coconut cream mixture. Mix well and set aside.

3. If using a blender, add all the ingredients, including the coconut cream and milk, and puree. Transfer to a mixing bowl and set aside.

4. Stored in a glass jar with a tight-fitting lid, the marinade will keep overnight in the refrigerator.

Satay

1 pound boneless, skinless chicken
breasts or thighs or pork loin
10 to 12 bamboo skewers, soaked
in water for 30 minutes, then
dried
⅓ cup pineapple juice
Vegetable oil spray

Makes 10 to 12 skewers

Make the Satay

5. Slice the chicken, if using, diagonally across the grain into thin strips approximately ¹⁄₁₀ inch wide, or as thin as possible. Or, for pork, slice the loin lengthwise in half, then slice diagonally across the grain, like the chicken. Add the meat to the marinade, mix well, coating it thoroughly, and let sit for 30 minutes.

6. Mound the charcoals in one side of the grill, leaving the other half empty. Heat the grill.

7. While waiting for the grill to get hot, thread 3 to 4 pieces of the chicken or pork onto each bamboo skewer into a tight bundle, covering 5 inches of the skewer. Add the pineapple juice to the marinade and mix well. Set aside.

8. Spray the skewers generously with vegetable oil. Lay the skewers with the meat portion on the grill over medium-high heat, arranging them very close to one another. (The uncovered portion of the skewers should not be over the coals.) Grill, brushing lightly and frequently with the marinade and pineapple juice mixture, and turning frequently to prevent burning, until the outside is crispy brown and the inside white and tender, 10 to 12 minutes. Transfer to a platter and serve immediately.

Malaysian-Style Lamb or Beef Satay

LAMB SATAY were my father's favorite. Although Thai street vendors seldom sell it, a Muslim restaurant across the street from my uncle's antique shop on New Road, in Bangkok, was where Papa went to get his fill. Top sirloin or flank steak can be substituted for the lamb. Serve with Indonesian Peanut Sauce (page 141) and/or Thai Sweet Pepper Sauce (page 142), and Indonesian-Style Cucumber Relish (page 152).

Make the Marinade

1. Put the coriander seeds in a small skillet and dry-roast, over medium-high heat, sliding the skillet back and forth over the burner to prevent burning, until the spice exudes a pleasant aroma, about 1 minute. Remove from the heat and transfer to a bowl to cool. Repeat with the cumin seeds. Grind in the spice grinder and set aside.

2. Pound the salt and garlic in a mortar with a pestle into a paste. One at a time, add the ginger, coriander seeds, cumin seeds, cayenne, turmeric, shallots, and peanuts, in sequence, adding each one after the previous ingredient has been incorporated into the paste. Transfer to a mixing bowl, add the tamarind juice, and mix well. Set aside.

3. Or, if using a blender, add all the ingredients, including the oil, and puree into a paste. Transfer to a mixing bowl and set aside.

4. Stored in a glass jar with a tight-fitting lid, the marinade will keep for a week in the refrigerator.

Marinade

Makes ½ cup

1 teaspoon coriander seeds
1 teaspoon cumin seeds
½ teaspoon sea salt
4 garlic cloves, minced
　(2 tablespoons)
1 teaspoon minced ginger
1 teaspoon cayenne pepper
1 teaspoon turmeric powder
2 shallots, minced (¼ cup)
2 tablespoons unsalted dry-
　roasted peanuts, ground
¼ cup tamarind juice
　(see page 137)
1 tablespoon vegetable oil
　(if using a blender)

Satay

1 pound boneless leg of lamb,
    top sirloin beef, or flank steak
16 to 18 bamboo skewers, soaked
    in water for 30 minutes, then
    dried
One 3-ounce can pineapple juice
Vegetable oil spray

Makes 16 to 18 skewers

Make the Satay

5. Slice the meat diagonally across the grain into strips approximately $\frac{1}{10}$ inch wide, or as thin as possible. Add to the bowl with the marinade. Mix well, coating the meat thoroughly. Cover and let sit for an hour—or, for best results, transfer to a zippered plastic bag and refrigerate overnight. Bring to room temperature before grilling.

6. Mound the charcoals in one side of the grill, leaving the other side empty. Heat the grill.

7. While waiting for the grill to get hot, thread 4 to 5 pieces of the lamb onto each bamboo skewer into a tight bundle, covering 5 inches of the skewer. Add the pineapple juice to the bowl of marinade and mix well. Set aside.

8. Spray the meat generously with the vegetable oil. Lay the skewers on the grill over medium-high heat, arranging the skewers very close to one another. (The uncovered portion of the skewers should not be over the coals.) Grill, brushing lightly and frequently with the marinade and pineapple juice mixture and turning frequently, for 3 to 4 minutes for medium-rare, or 5 to 6 minutes for well done. Transfer to a platter and serve piping hot.

Thai-Style Chicken Satay

FOR CENTURIES spice trading brought culinary, social, religious, and political exchanges between the kingdoms of Siam (Thailand) and Java. Today, satay are so much a part of Thai cooking that it's hard to believe they were once strictly an Indonesian dish. Serve with Thai Sweet Pepper Sauce (page 142) or Thai Vegetarian Peanut Sauce (page 143).

Make the Marinade

1. Put the coriander seeds in a small skillet and dry-roast over medium-high heat, sliding the skillet back and forth over the burner to prevent burning, until the seeds exude a pleasant aroma, about 1 minute. Remove from the heat and transfer to a bowl to cool. Repeat with the cumin seeds. Grind in a spice grinder and set aside.

2. Pound the salt and garlic in a mortar with a pestle into a paste. Add the galangal and pound into a paste. Transfer to a mixing bowl and add the coriander and cumin seeds, cayenne, and turmeric powder. Mix to combine. Add the coconut cream mixture and mix well. Set aside.

3. Or, if using a blender, add all the ingredients and puree. Transfer to a mixing bowl and set aside.

4. Stored in a glass jar with a tight-fitting lid, the marinade will keep overnight in the refrigerator.

Marinade

Makes ⅔ cup

1 teaspoon coriander seeds
1 teaspoon cumin seeds
½ teaspoon sea salt
5 garlic cloves, minced
   (2½ tablespoons)
1 tablespoon minced galangal
   or ginger
1 teaspoon cayenne pepper
½ teaspoon turmeric powder
½ cup combined coconut cream
   and milk (the consistency of
   whole milk) (see page 135)

Satay

1 pound boneless, skinless chicken
   breasts or thighs
10 to 12 bamboo skewers, soaked
   in water for 30 minutes, then
   dried
Vegetable oil spray

Makes 10 to 12 skewers

Make the Satay

5. Slice the chicken diagonally across the grain into thin strips approximately $1/10$ inch, or as thin as possible. Add the chicken to the marinade; mix well to coat. Cover and refrigerate for 30 minutes.

6. Mound the charcoals in one side of the grill, leaving the other side empty. Heat the grill.

7. While waiting for the grill to get hot, thread 3 to 4 pieces of the chicken onto each bamboo skewer into a tight bundle, covering 5 inches of the skewer. Reserve the remaining marinade.

8. Spray the chicken generously with vegetable oil. Lay the skewers with the chicken portion on the grill over medium-high heat, arranging them very close to one another. (The uncovered portion of the skewers should not be over the coals.) Grill, basting frequently with the marinade and turning frequently to prevent burning, until the surface is crispy and brown and the inside is firm and white, 8 to 10 minutes. Transfer to a platter and serve.

Shrimp Satay

SATAY FROM SOUTHERN THAILAND are the most flavorful, because of the close proximity to Malaysia, where satay marinades, like all Malaysian cooking, are enhanced with an abundance of dried herbs and spices.

Serve with Thai Sweet Pepper Sauce (page 142) and Thai-Style Cucumber Relish (page 151).

Make the Marinade

1. Put the peppercorns in a small skillet and dry-roast over medium-high heat, sliding the skillet back and forth over the burner to prevent burning, until the spice exudes a pleasant aroma, about 1 minute. Remove from the heat and transfer to a bowl to cool. Repeat with the coriander seeds. Grind in a spice grinder and set aside.

2. Combine the garlic, peppercorns and coriander seeds, ginger, cayenne, salt, basil, and soy sauce in a bowl and mix well. Add the oil and mix again to combine. Set aside.

3. Stored in a glass jar with a tight-fitting lid, the marinade will keep for a week in the refrigerator.

Make the Satay

4. Add the shrimp to the marinade and mix well to coat. Cover and refrigerate for at least 20 minutes, but no longer than 1 hour.

5. Mound the charcoal in one side of the grill, leaving the other side empty. Heat the grill.

6. While waiting for the grill to get hot, remove the shrimp from the refrigerator. Thread a shrimp from the tail through the body to the head onto a bamboo skewer, adding 3 to 4 shrimp to each skewer. Repeat with the remaining shrimp.

7. Spray the shrimp generously with vegetable oil. Lay the skewers with the shrimp portion on the grill over medium-high heat, arranging them very close to one another. (The uncovered portion of the skewers should not be over the coals.) Grill, turning frequently to prevent burning and brushing with the reserved marinade, until the shrimp are pink and firm, 3 to 4 minutes. Transfer to a platter and serve.

Marinade

Makes ¼ cup

1 teaspoon white peppercorns
1 teaspoon coriander seeds
4 garlic cloves, minced
    (2 tablespoons)
1 teaspoon minced ginger
1 teaspoon cayenne pepper
¼ teaspoon sea salt
⅓ cup Thai basil or mint leaves,
    minced
2 tablespoons soy sauce
2 tablespoons vegetable oil

Satay

1 pound large shrimp, peeled,
    deveined, and dried
    thoroughly
16 to 18 bamboo skewers,
    soaked in water for 30
    minutes, then dried
Vegetable oil spray

Makes 16 to 18 skewers

Tofu Satay

I LEARNED TO MAKE this recipe after tasting it at Whole Earth, a vegetarian restaurant in Chiang Mai, Thailand.

Firm, oblong-shaped cakes of tofu, with most of the water extracted, are best. To extract the water, remove the tofu from the package and set it between two plates, with a weight (two cans, for instance) on the top for a couple of hours. Discard the water. Serve with Thai Vegetarian Peanut Sauce (page 143) and Burmese Cucumber Relish (page 153).

Marinade

Makes 1¼ cups

1 teaspoon white peppercorns
½ teaspoon sea salt
4 garlic cloves, minced
   (2 tablespoons)
1 tablespoon Madras curry
   powder
1 teaspoon cayenne pepper
2 tablespoons soy sauce
½ cup coconut cream
   (see page 135)

Satay

One 16-ounce package very
   firm tofu
9 bamboo skewers, soaked in
   water for 30 minutes, then
   dried
Vegetable oil spray

Makes 9 skewers

Make the Marinade

1. Put the peppercorns in a skillet and dry-roast over medium-high heat, sliding the skillet back and forth to prevent burning, until the peppercorns exude a pleasant aroma, about 1 minute. Remove from the heat and transfer to a bowl to cool. Grind in a spice grinder and set aside.

2. Combine the salt, garlic, peppercorns, curry powder, and cayenne in a bowl and mix well. Add the soy sauce and coconut cream and stir to combine. Set aside.

3. Stored in a glass jar with a tight-fitting lid, the marinade will keep overnight in the refrigerator.

Make the Satay

4. Slice the tofu crosswise approximately ½ inch thick. Put in a bowl and cover with the marinade. Mix gently to coat the tofu, trying not to break up the pieces. Let marinate for 30 minutes.

5. Mound the charcoal in one side of the grill, leaving the other side empty. Heat the grill.

6. While waiting for the grill to get hot, thread a bamboo skewer lengthwise, through the center of a tofu slice. Repeat with the remaining tofu, placing two pieces of tofu on each skewer. Transfer the remaining marinade to a small bowl and set aside.

7. Spray the tofu generously with vegetable oil. Lay the skewers with the tofu portion on the grill over medium-high heat, arranging them very close to one another. (The uncovered portion of the skewers should not be over the coals.) Grill, basting with the reserved marinade and turning frequently, until the tofu is crispy and brown, about 6 minutes. Transfer to a platter and serve.

Chicken Tandoori

AUTHENTIC INDIAN TANDOORI requires a special clay oven with a wood or charcoal fire. Whole chickens coated in herbs and spices are suspended on a hook inside the oven to cook. No tandoori oven? No problem. Use boneless chicken pieces instead of the whole bird. I add a handful of dried coconut husks or mesquite chips to the fire during the smoking process.

Garam masala and ghee (clarified butter) can be bought in Indian and Middle Eastern markets. To make your own garam masala, refer to the recipe on page 139. Serve the chicken with Raita (page 150).

1. In a blender or food processor, combine the garlic, ginger, garam masala, cayenne, paprika, turmeric powder, salt, yogurt, and lemon juice. Blend to a smooth paste. Transfer the mixture to a large zippered plastic bag.

2. Score the surface of chicken pieces lightly and add to the bag. Seal and toss the bag back and forth to coat the chicken thoroughly. Refrigerate for at least 1 hour, but no longer than 4 hours.

3. Soak a handful of mesquite wood chips or coconut husks in a bowl of water. Heat the grill. While waiting for the grill to get hot, spray the metal skewers with vegetable oil. Remove the chicken from the refrigerator and thread a couple of pieces of chicken onto each skewer. Transfer the remaining marinade to a bowl and set aside. Mound the charcoals in one side of the grill, leaving the other side empty. Generously spray the chicken with vegetable oil, and lay the skewers on the rack directly over the hot coals. Sear the chicken for 10 seconds, then flip the skewers over to sear the other side for another 10 seconds. Do this a couple of times, until the outside is slightly charred. Baste with the reserved marinade and move the skewers to the side of the grill without coals. Sprinkle the soaked mesquite chips or coconut husks onto the hot coals. Cover the grill and grill-smoke for 3 minutes. Be sure to open all vents in the top of the grill cover. Uncover, baste the chicken with the marinade and the ghee, turn and baste again. Cover and cook, basting and turning every 3 minutes, until the chicken is golden, about 12 minutes in all. Transfer to a platter and serve.

4 garlic cloves, minced
  (2 tablespoons)
¼ cup minced ginger
1½ teaspoons garam masala
  (see page 139)
1 teaspoon cayenne pepper
1 teaspoon paprika
½ teaspoon turmeric powder
½ teaspoon sea salt
1 cup plain yogurt
¼ cup fresh lemon juice
2 pounds boneless, skinless chicken
  breasts and thighs
4 to 5 flat metal skewers
Vegetable oil spray
2 tablespoons ghee (clarified
  butter)

Makes 6 servings

Chicken Yakitori

I ADD A LITTLE cayenne pepper to these traditional Japanese skewers. Daikon, an Asian radish, tenderizes the meat. Serve with Ponzu Sauce (page 148) and Chayote Relish (page 155).

⅓ cup mirin (sweet rice wine)

⅓ cup sake

2 tablespoons soy sauce

⅓ cup pureed daikon

1 tablespoon sugar

1 teaspoon cayenne pepper

1 tablespoon vegetable oil

1½ pounds boneless, skinless chicken breasts or thighs, cut into 1-inch cubes

9 to 12 bamboo skewers, soaked in water for 30 minutes, then dried

Vegetable oil spray

Makes 9 to 12 skewers

1. Combine the mirin, sake, soy sauce, daikon, sugar, cayenne, and vegetable oil in a large zippered plastic bag. Seal and toss the bag back and forth to mix the ingredients. Add the chicken pieces, seal, and toss the bag back and forth until all the chicken pieces are coated with the marinade. Refrigerate for 30 minutes to 1 hour.

2. Mound the charcoals in one side of the grill, leaving the other side empty. Heat the grill.

3. While waiting for for the grill to get hot, remove the chicken from the refrigerator. Thread 5 to 6 pieces of chicken close to one another onto each bamboo skewer. Transfer the remaining marinade to a bowl and set aside.

4. Spray the chicken pieces generously with vegetable oil, and lay the skewers on the grill over medium-high heat. (The uncovered portion of the skewers should not be over the coals.) Grill, turning frequently to prevent burning and basting with the reserved marinade, until the chicken is slightly charred, and the inside is white, about 12 minutes. Transfer to a platter and serve.

Mongolian-Chinese-Style Lamb Kebabs

GENGHIS KHAN INVADED China in 1211, and the Mongols remained in power until 1368. Today, some Mongol influences remain in Chinese cooking, particularly Mongol-style barbecue. The marinade for this recipe is thickened with eggs and flour. Before grilling, sesame seeds are dusted over the lamb, adding a unique, crispy nutty surface to the meat. Serve with Tomato and Chile Sambal (page 146) and Chinese Flatbread with Scallions (page 115) or warm pita bread.

1. Put the white peppercorns in a small skillet and dry-roast, over medium-high heat, sliding the skillet back and forth over the burner to prevent burning, until the spice exudes a pleasant aroma, about 1 minute. Remove from the heat and transfer to a bowl to cool. Repeat with the Szechwan peppercorns. Grind in a spice grinder and set aside.

2. Combine the beaten eggs with the flour in a medium bowl. Mix lightly, then add the salt, peppercorns, tomato sauce, soy sauce, rice wine, and sesame oil and mix well. Add the ginger and scallions, stir to combine. Transfer the mixture to a large zippered plastic bag. Add the lamb, seal the bag securely, and toss it back and forth to coat the lamb well. Refrigerate for at least 1 hour, or, for best results, overnight.

3. Mound the coals in one side of the grill, leaving the other side empty. Heat the grill.

4. Spray the metal skewers with vegetable oil. Spread the sesame seeds in a pie plate. Remove the lamb from the refrigerator and roll the cubes in the seeds. Shake off all the excess seeds and thread 4 to 5 lamb cubes close to one another onto each metal skewer.

5. Spray the lamb with vegetable oil, and lay the skewers onto the rack directly over the hot coals. Turn frequently until the outside is slightly charred, then, still turning frequently, cook for 2 to 3 minutes longer. If the lamb sticks to the grill, gently remove it from the grill and spray with vegetable oil. Or if there are shooting flames, remove the skewers and douse the flames with water. Move the skewers to the empty side of the grill, cover the grill, and grill-smoke. Open the air vents in the top of the grill cover. Uncover and turn the skewers every 3 minutes, for 11 to 12 minutes in all for medium-rare lamb. Transfer to a platter and serve.

1 teaspoon white peppercorns
1 tablespoon Szechwan peppercorns
2 large eggs, slightly beaten
¾ cup all-purpose flour
½ teaspoon sea salt
1 cup tomato sauce
¼ cup soy sauce
3 tablespoons Chinese rice wine (Shaoxing) or dry vermouth
1 teaspoon sesame oil
¼ cup minced ginger
5 scallions (white and green parts), minced (¾ cup)
2 pounds boneless leg of lamb, cut into 1½-inch cubes
1½ cups sesame seeds
10 to 12 metal skewers
Vegetable oil spray

Makes 10 to 12 skewers

Char Siew – Chinese Barbecued Pork

THIS SUCCULENT MEAT is traditionally cooked hanging on hooks inside a smoking barbecue oven. This easier and faster method cooks the pork on a charcoal grill.

Serve as a main course with Chile and Soy Sambal (page 147) and Chinese Flatbread with Scallions (page 115). Char siew can be sliced and used as a garnish over rice or noodles, or stir-fried with vegetables.

½ cup sugar
1 star anise
1 teaspoon cinnamon
1 teaspoon freshly ground white
    pepper
½ teaspoon sea salt
¼ cup Chinese rice wine (Shaoxing)
    or dry vermouth
One 6-ounce can pineapple juice
1 tablespoon dark soy sauce
1 tablespoon soy sauce
1 teaspoon sesame oil
2 pounds pork tenderloin, sliced
    lengthwise into 1½-inch-wide
    strips
8 metal skewers
Vegetable oil spray

Makes 8 skewers

1. In a large zippered plastic bag, combine the sugar, star anise, cinnamon, pepper, salt, wine, pineapple juice, soy sauces, and sesame oil. Seal the bag and shake to mix. Add the pork, seal and toss the bag back and forth to coat the pork slices. Refrigerate for at least 1 hour or, for best results, overnight.

2. Soak a handful of mesquite chips or cinnamon sticks in a bowl of water. Heat the grill.

3. While waiting for the grill to get hot, remove the pork from the refrigerator. Thread 4 to 5 pieces of pork onto each skewer. Repeat with the remaining pork. Transfer the remaining marinade to a bowl and set aside.

4. Rake the hot coals into a mound on one side of the grill. Spray the pork generously with vegetable oil and lay the skewers on the rack directly over the hot coals. Sear the meat for a minute or two. Baste with the marinade and turn the skewers over. Repeat once or twice, or until the outside is slightly charred. Baste with the marinade and move the skewers to the empty side of the grill.

5. Sprinkle the soaked mesquite or cinnamon sticks over the charcoal. Cover the grill and grill-smoke. Be sure to open the air vents in the top of the grill cover. Uncover the grill and baste the meat every 3 minutes, until the pork is cooked through, 11 to 12 minutes in all.

6. Cool for 5 minutes before removing the pork from the skewers. Slice into thin bite-sized pieces and serve.

Bulgogi – Korean Barbecued Beef

WITH ITS SPICE-SCENTED meat and lightly sweet flavor, Korean barbecue reminds me, in a way, of char siew, Chinese barbecued pork. It's fun to serve Korean barbecue because of the array of pickles and salads that accompany the grilled meat. These are available ready-made in Korean and some other Asian markets. Even without them, you can still enjoy an authentic Korean meal with Grilled Potato, Egg, and Bean Thread Salad (page 91) (or even an American-style potato salad) and the popular kim-chi, spicy pickled cabbage and daikon, which is available in many supermarkets, as well as Asian markets.

Traditional Korean bulgogi uses beef or pork shortribs, thinly sliced across the bones. This is a difficult cut to get in American supermarkets, so I use beef sirloin as a substitute.

1. Slice the beef diagonally across the grain into long thin strips approximately ¼ inch thick. Set aside.

2. Combine the scallions, ginger, garlic, sesame seeds, sugar, pepper, cayenne, molasses, lemon juice, soy sauce, and sesame oil in a bowl and mix well. Transfer to a large zippered plastic bag and add the beef slices. Seal and toss the bag lightly back and forth to coat the beef. Refrigerate overnight.

3. Heat the grill.

4. While waiting for the grill to get hot, remove the beef from the refrigerator. Spray the metal skewers with vegetable oil and thread a slice of beef lengthwise onto a skewer, keeping it flat. Add 1 or 2 more pieces of the beef to the skewer. Repeat with the remaining beef. Transfer the remaining marinade to a bowl.

5. Generously spray the beef with vegetable oil. Lay the skewers on the grill over medium-high heat. Grill, basting the beef with the reserved marinade and turning frequently to prevent burning, until medium-rare, 3 to 4 minutes. Transfer to a plate and remove the beef from the skewers.

6. Slice the beef into bite-sized pieces. Transfer to a serving platter lined with lettuce leaves, garnish with the lemon slices, and serve.

1½ pounds beef sirloin
4 scallions (white and green parts), minced
2 tablespoons minced ginger
4 garlic cloves, minced (2 tablespoons)
2 tablespoons sesame seeds
3 tablespoons sugar
1 teaspoon freshly ground black pepper
1 teaspoon cayenne pepper
1 tablespoon molasses
¼ cup fresh lemon juice
¼ cup soy sauce
2 tablespoons sesame oil
10 to 12 long metal skewers
Vegetable oil spray
10 to 12 romaine lettuce leaves
1 lemon, thinly sliced

Makes 10 to 12 skewers

Moo Ping – Grilled Pork Strips

MOO PING IS COOKED over small charcoal grills and sold early in the morning and late in the afternoon in northern Thailand and Laos, and is eaten as breakfast, a snack, or for dinner. Traditionally, thick bamboo tubes are split and pared down into long paper-thin strips, and the pieces of savory pork are pressed between two bamboo strips and tied securely with twine, then grilled. Bamboo skewers work just as well. Serve with Fruit Ambrosia (page 156).

1. Slice the pork diagonally across the grain into strips approximately ⅓ inch thick, 1 inch wide, and 3 inches long. Set aside.

2. Combine the lemongrass, garlic, oyster sauce, sugar, and pepper in a large zippered plastic bag. Seal the bag and toss it back and forth to combine. Add the pork strips, seal, and toss the bag back and forth several times to coat the pork strips with the marinade. Refrigerate for at least 1 hour, or, for best results, overnight.

3. Mound the charcoal in one side of the grill, leaving the other side empty. Heat the grill.

4. While waiting for the grill to get hot, remove the pork from the refrigerator. Thread a piece of pork lengthwise onto a skewer, keeping it flat. Add 1 to 2 more pieces of the pork to the skewer. Repeat with the remaining pork. Transfer the remaining marinade to a bowl and add the pineapple juice. Mix well and set aside.

5. Generously spray the pork with vegetable oil. Lay the skewers on the grill over medium-high heat, arranging them close together. (The uncovered portion of the skewers should not be over the coals.) Grill, basting with the marinade and flipping frequently, until the outer sides are slightly charred and the pork is firm to the touch; cooked for 3 to 4 minutes. Transfer to a platter and serve.

1 pound pork tenderloin
1 stalk lemongrass, tough outer layers and green parts removed, minced
5 garlic cloves, minced (2½ tablespoons)
¼ cup oyster sauce
1 tablespoon sugar
1 teaspoon freshly ground black pepper
9 bamboo skewers, soaked in water for 30 minutes, then dried
One 6-ounce can pineapple juice
Vegetable oil spray

Makes 9 skewers

Salt-Grilled Yellowtail Tuna

THE JAPANESE TECHNIQUE of salt-grilling begins by covering the fish entirely in salt for a couple of hours. Then the salt is removed, and the fish rinsed and dried. The process firms up the flesh of the fish while keeping the grilled fish moist. The cooked fish smells slightly like the salt air at the seashore. Coarse sea salt can be found in most supermarkets. Katsuo mirin furikake, a seasoned dried bonito and sesame seed mix, is a Japanese seasoning mix used for rice and soup; it is available in Asian markets. Serve with steamed Japanese rice (see page 105) and Wasabi Mayonnaise (page 145).

2 cups coarse sea salt
2 pounds yellowtail or albacore tuna, rinsed and patted dry
¼ cup olive oil
2 tablespoons katsuo mirin furikake (seasoned dried bonito and sesame seed mix)
1 teaspoon freshly ground white pepper
¼ cup chopped parsley, coarsely chopped
8 bamboo skewers, soaked in water for 30 minutes, then dried
2 lemons, thinly sliced
Vegetable oil spray

Makes 6 to 8 skewers

1. Place a wire rack in a baking pan. Pour the salt onto a plate and coat the tuna generously with it. Transfer the tuna to the rack and set aside for 25 minutes.

2. Combine the oil, katsuo mirin furikake, pepper, and parsley in a bowl. Mix well and set aside.

3. Mound the charcoal in one side of the grill, leaving the other side empty. Heat the grill.

4. While waiting for the grill to get hot, rinse the salt off the tuna with cool water. Pat the tuna dry and cut into 1-inch cubes. Add to the bowl with the oil mixture and coat well. Thread 4 to 5 pieces of tuna close together onto each bamboo skewer, alternating the tuna with the lemon slices. Repeat with the remaining tuna and lemon slices.

5. Generously spray the tuna with vegetable oil. Lay the skewers on the grill over medium-high heat. (The uncovered portion of the skewers should not be over the coals.) Grill, turning frequently to prevent burning, until slightly charred, about 4 minutes for medium-rare, 5 to 6 minutes for well-done. Transfer to a platter and serve.

Garlic-and-Pepper Shrimp and Kumquats

SALT, GARLIC, AND WHITE peppercorns are a classic Thai combination used for grilling seafood. Each year when my favorite fruit the kumquat ripens, covering the small tree in my companion Italo's studio, I make preserves, chutneys, and this favorite of mine. Grilled kumquats are so good that I grill extra skewers of kumquats only. If kumquats are unavailable, substitute thick lemon or lime slices.

1. Snip the fins from the shrimp with scissors. Using the scissors, cut the shells open down the back. Remove the dark vein from each shrimp and rinse them with cool water. Put the shrimp in a strainer, sprinkle 1 tablespoon of the salt over them, and massage lightly; let sit for 5 to 10 minutes.

2. Rinse the shrimp again with cool water, and pat dry with paper towels. Set aside.

3. Put the peppercorns in a small skillet and dry-roast over medium-high heat, sliding the skillet back and forth to prevent burning, until the peppercorns exude a pleasant aroma, about 1 minute. Remove from the heat and transfer to a bowl. Let cool, then grind in a spice grinder. Set aside.

4. Combine the garlic, cilantro, peppercorns, sugar, the remaining ¼ teaspoon salt, and the fish sauce in a bowl; mix well. Add the shrimp, and toss. Cover and refrigerate for 30 minutes.

5. Mound the charcoals in one side of the grill, leaving the other side empty, heat the grill.

6. While waiting for the grill to get hot, remove the shrimp from the refrigerator. Remove the shrimp from the marinade, shaking off the excess marinade, and set the marinade aside. Thread a shrimp

24 large shrimp in the shell
1 tablespoon plus ¼ teaspoon sea salt
1 tablespoon white peppercorns
1 head garlic, separated into cloves, peeled, and coarsely chopped (approximately ½ cup)
1 tablespoon minced cilantro stems (without leaves)
1 teaspoon sugar
1 tablespoon fish sauce (nam pla)
8 bamboo skewers, soaked in water for 30 minutes, then dried
8 kumquats, sliced crosswise in half and seeded
Vegetable oil spray
3 tablespoons vegetable oil
2 to 3 serrano chiles, slivered

Makes 8 skewers

lengthwise onto a bamboo skewer, from the head end through the tail, then thread a sliced kumquat onto the skewer close to the shrimp, and repeat so that the skewer has 3 shrimp and 2 kumquat halves. Repeat with the remaining shrimp and kumquats.

7. Generously spray the shrimp with vegetable oil and lay the skewers on the grill over medium-low heat. (The uncovered portion of the skewers should not be over the coals.) Grill, turning frequently to prevent burning, until the shells are slightly charred and crispy and the shrimp are pink, 5 to 6 minutes. Transfer to a platter and tent with aluminum foil to keep warm.

8. Heat the vegetable oil in a skillet over high heat for 1 to 2 minutes. Add the reserved marinade and the chiles and stir constantly until the garlic turns golden, about 3 minutes. Remove from the heat.

9. Remove the shrimp and kumquats from the skewers and place on a platter. Pour the sauce over them and serve.

Seared Tuna with Wasabi-Miso Marinade

THE MARINADE MAKES a crisp crust when the tuna is grilled. The wasabi is spicy, but its pungency is tempered by the saltiness of miso. Serve with Wasabi Mayonnaise (page 145).

3 tablespoons sesame seeds
2 tablespoons wasabi powder
2 tablespoons red miso
1 large egg yolk
⅓ cup mirin (sweet rice wine)
⅓ cup sake
1 tablespoon soy sauce
1 teaspoon sesame oil
2 tablespoons minced ginger
2 pounds tuna, cut into 1-inch
    cubes
6 to 8 bamboo skewers, soaked
    in water for 30 minutes, then
    dried
Vegetable oil spray

Makes 6 to 8 skewers

1. Put the sesame seeds in a small skillet and dry-roast over medium heat, sliding the skillet back and forth to prevent burning, until the seeds are slightly golden, about 1 minute. Remove from the heat and transfer to a bowl to cool.

2. Grind the seeds in a spice grinder to a powder. Transfer to a bowl and add the wasabi powder, red miso, and egg yolk. Beat with a fork to blend well. Add the mirin, sake, soy sauce, sesame oil, and ginger. Stir to mix well. Transfer the mixture to a large zippered plastic bag and add the tuna. Seal and toss the bag back and forth to coat the tuna. Refrigerate for 30 minutes.

3. Mound the charcoal in one side of the grill, leaving the other side empty. Heat the grill.

4. While waiting for the grill to get hot, remove the tuna from the refrigerator. Thread 3 to 4 pieces of tuna close to one another onto each bamboo skewer. Repeat with the remaining tuna. Transfer the remaining marinade to a bowl.

5. Spray the tuna generously with vegetable oil and place the skewers on the grill over medium-high heat. (The uncovered portion of the skewers should not be over the coals.) Grill, turning frequently to prevent burning, and brushing alternately with the marinade and vegetable oil, until the outside is slightly charred, about 4 minutes for medium-rare, 5 to 6 minutes for well-done. Transfer to a platter and serve.

Grilled Shrimp on Sugarcane Stalks

YEARS AGO when Vietnamese immigrants first arrived in San Diego, I befriended Toey, a Vietnamese woman who had opened a small grocery store. She taught me how to use sugarcane as skewers when grilling shrimp. Serve with Vietnamese Sweet-and-Sour Sauce with Tamarind Juice (page 149).

1. Put the rice in a small skillet and dry-roast over high heat, sliding the skillet back and forth over the burner to prevent burning, until the rice grains are golden, 1 to 2 minutes. Remove from the heat and transfer to a bowl, let cool, then grind to a powder in a coffee or spice grinder. Set aside.

2. Combine the shrimp, garlic, ginger, sugar, salt, pepper, and rice powder in a food processor. Process until the ingredients form a ball. With the machine running, add the egg whites and process to a paste. Transfer to a bowl.

3. Heat the grill.

4. While waiting for the grill to get hot, line a tray with wax paper and spray it with vegetable oil. Spray your hands with vegetable oil. Pick up 2 to 3 tablespoons of the shrimp mixture, and put it around the upper half of a sugarcane strip, molding it into an oval shape (like a corn dog). Repeat with the remaining shrimp.

5. Spray the shrimp mixture generously with vegetable oil. Place the skewers on the grill over medium-low heat, turning frequently to prevent burning, until the shrimp mixture is slightly charred and firm to the touch, 4 to 5 minutes. Transfer to a serving platter.

6. Fill a large bowl with lukewarm water. Invite your guests to serve themselves: To eat, bathe a rice paper in the water, shake off the excess water, and set the rice paper on a plate to soften briefly. Line the rice paper with a couple of pieces of lettuce, cucumber, cilantro sprigs, and mint leaf. Break the shrimp off the sugarcane into bite-sized pieces and put on top of the herbs. Fold the bottom edge of the rice paper over the filling, then roll the rice paper over the filling from left to right, forming a cylinder. Dip in the sauce and chew on the sugarcane between bites.

1 tablespoon Thai long-grain jasmine rice

2 pounds shrimp, peeled, deveined, rinsed, and thoroughly dried

3 garlic cloves, minced

1 tablespoon minced ginger

1 teaspoon sugar

½ teaspoon sea salt

½ teaspoon freshly ground white pepper

2 large egg whites, slightly beaten

Three 8-inch pieces sugarcane, peeled and quartered lengthwise

Vegetable oil spray

Twelve 9-inch round rice papers

8 to 10 red or green leaf lettuce leaves torn into bite-sized pieces

1 cucumber, peeled, seeded, and cut into 10 long thin pieces

12 to 15 cilantro sprigs

12 to 15 mint leaves

Makes 12 skewers

Wrapped and Grilled

THE CHILD OF ESAN is an autobiographical novel written in 1976 by Kampoon Boontawee, who was born and raised in Buri Rum, a province in northeast Thailand. The book is about a poor farmer and his family living through a terrible drought there. On the verge of starvation, the family walks to a distant village by the river, hoping to catch enough fish to make fermented fish that will last for years. They live on wild game and food that others share with them. Traveling light, without cooking or eating implements, they cook whatever they can scavenge, seasoning their food with the fermented fish and chiles, wrapping everything in banana or teak leaves, and grilling the pouches over a fire.

Today, Thailand is a modern Westernized nation, yet many people in rural provinces still wrap and grill their food as in the novel. The same is true in rural areas of Laos, Myanmar (Burma), and Cambodia. Whole or sliced fish, baby shrimp, buffalo and pork, and rice and vegetables are wrapped in banana leaves, and bamboo leaves and tubes, which grow wild everywhere.

Other Asian cuisines use the same technique. Banana and pandanus leaves are used in southern India. The Japanese are known for salt-grilling fish. In Huroko-style Japanese grilling, the food is covered with pine needles and grilled between two plates. In China, bamboo tubes and leaves are popular for wrapping.

My mother used dried bamboo leaves, which she soaked in water and then filled with sticky rice and seasoned meat. When these were grilled, the outer layer of rice became crunchy, and the filling acquired a smoky aroma and a nutty taste and chewy texture.

The following recipes use fresh or frozen banana and pandanus leaves, dried corn husks, and dried bamboo leaves. When using aluminum foil as a wrap, I line it with leaves. This gives the grilled food a pleasant aroma and prevents the metallic taste.

Fresh and frozen banana leaves can be purchased in Asian supermarkets. Thaw frozen banana leaves at room temperature, then wash with a cloth using soap and water, rinse, and dry thoroughly. Cut away the hard stem along one of the edges and discard. Then cut the leaves to the specified size called for in the recipe.

Fresh leaves must be softened before using. To do this, fan both sides of each leaf over a low gas flame, or place the leaves directly on top of an electric burner for a couple of seconds. In Asia, freshly cut leaves are softened in the sun.

Frozen banana leaves will keep for months. Once the leaves have been thawed and washed, they should be stored in a zippered plastic bag in the refrigerator, where they will keep for 1 to 2 weeks.

Fresh and frozen pandanus leaves, used in Southeast Asia and India, are long broad dark-green leaves that exude a sweet yet musty scent when cooked. Fresh and frozen pandanus leaves are available in Asian markets. Thaw, wash, and dry thoroughly before using. Whether bought fresh or frozen, pandanus leaves can be stored in a zippered plastic bag in the freezer for several months.

Dried corn husks are most commonly used for Mexican tamales. They can be purchased in major supermarkets or Latin American markets. Before using, soften them in lukewarm water for 20 minutes, then drain and dry thoroughly. Store dried corn husks in a zippered plastic bag in the pantry. They will keep for a long time.

Dried bamboo leaves are sold in bundles in Asian markets. Soak them in cool water for 30 minutes, wash lightly with soap and water, and dry thoroughly before using. Wrapped in plastic, dried bamboo leaves will keep in the pantry for months.

Aluminum foil makes tight and sturdy packages for grilling, but I am uncertain of the effects of placing highly seasoned food in direct contact with aluminum over intense heat, and I don't like the metallic taste foil can impart either. My solution is to line the foil with aromatic leaves, shielding the food.

Grilled Chicken in Pandanus Leaves

IN THAILAND, wrapped chicken is deep-fried, rather than grilled. I prefer to grill, for moister meat with less grease. Soaked dried corn husks can be used in place of the pandanus leaves. Serve with Thai Sweet Pepper Sauce (page 142).

1. Put the peppercorns in a small skillet and dry-roast over medium-high heat, sliding the skillet back and forth over the burner to prevent burning, until the peppercorns exude a pleasant aroma, about 1 minute. Remove from the heat and transfer to a bowl to cool.

2. Grind the peppercorns in a spice grinder and transfer to a large zippered plastic bag. Add the sugar, salt, garlic, soy sauce, oyster sauce, lemon juice, and sesame oil. Seal the bag and toss gently back and forth to combine. Add the chicken pieces. Seal and toss several times to coat. Refrigerate for at least 30 minutes and up to 4 hours.

3. Heat the grill.

4. While waiting for the coals to get hot, wrap 1 to 2 pieces of chicken in each pandanus leaf and secure with a toothpick.

5. Rake the hot coals into a mound on one side of the grill. Generously spray the pandanus bundles with water and place on the rack directly over the hot coals. Grill, turning frequently to prevent burning, until the leaves are slightly charred, 2 to 3 minutes. If the leaves start to burn, spray with water. Move the bundles to the empty side of the grill, cover, and grill-smoke for about 7 minutes. Be sure to open the air vents in the top of the grill cover. Test for doneness by piercing a bundle with a knife: the juices should run clear. Transfer to a serving platter and let rest for 5 minutes.

6. Unwrap the chicken, discard the leaves, and serve.

1 teaspoon white peppercorns
1 tablespoon sugar
1 teaspoon sea salt
9 garlic cloves, minced (¼ cup)
⅓ cup soy sauce
2 tablespoons oyster sauce
2 tablespoons fresh lemon juice
1 teaspoon sesame oil
2 pounds boneless, skinless chicken breasts or thighs, cut into 1-inch cubes
14 fresh or frozen pandanus leaves (see page 39), or 30 dried corn husks, soaked in water for 20 minutes, then dried
14 or 30 toothpicks, soaked in water for 30 minutes, then dried

Makes 6 to 7 servings

Myanmar Chicken

AS NEIGHBORS, Myanmar (Burma) and Thailand have a shared past with centuries of historic entanglements. It would make sense, then, that the cuisines of two countries shared similarities, but it isn't so. Myanmar food is simpler, with clean and distinct tastes compared to Thai dishes, which are layered with multiple flavors. This light and healthy recipe is an example of typical Myanmar cooking. Serve it with steamed Thai long-grain jasmine rice (see page 105) and Burmese Cucumber Relish (page 153).

1. Put the onion, garlic, ginger, lemongrass, paprika, turmeric powder, salt, lime juice, soy sauce, and fish sauce in a large zippered plastic bag. Seal and gently toss the bag back and forth. Add the chicken pieces, seal, and toss the bag back and forth to coat. Refrigerate for at least 1 hour, or overnight.

2. Heat the grill.

3. While waiting for the coals to get hot, remove the chicken from the refrigerator. Stack 2 pieces of banana leaves together, dull sides up and with the grains running horizontally. Put approximately ½ cup of the chicken in the center of the leaves. Pick up the edge of the leaves closest to you, and fold it over the filling, then pick up the opposite edge of the leaves and fold over. Flatten the pouch, securing each end with toothpicks. Repeat with the remaining leaves and chicken.

4. Rake the coals into a mound on one side of the grill. Put the banana pouches on the rack directly over the medium-hot coals. Spray lightly with water and grill, turning frequently to prevent burning, for 5 minutes. Move the pouches to the empty side of the grill, cover, and grill-smoke for another 7 to 8 minutes. Be sure to open the air vents in the top of the grill cover.

5. To check for doneness, undo one of the pouches: the chicken should be firm to the touch. Transfer to a platter.

6. Unwrap the pouches, discard the banana leaves, and serve.

1 small onion, minced (½ cup)
4 garlic cloves, minced
   (2 tablespoons)
1 tablespoon minced ginger
1 stalk lemongrass, tough outer
   layers and green parts removed,
   minced
1 teaspoon paprika
1 teaspoon turmeric powder
¼ teaspoon sea salt
2 tablespoons fresh lime juice
1 tablespoon soy sauce
1 tablespoon fish sauce (nam pla)
2 pounds boneless, skinless chicken
   breasts or thighs, sliced across
   the grain into ⅛-inch strips
1 package banana leaves, trimmed
   and cut into sixteen 9 × 12-inch
   pieces (see page 38)
16 toothpicks, soaked in water for
   30 minutes, then dried

Makes 8 servings

Chinese-Style Chicken in Bamboo Leaves

THESE POUCHES CAN BE PREPARED a day ahead for barbecues or picnics. Five-spice powder is available in Asian markets, or you can make your own (see page 140).

4 garlic cloves, minced
   (2 tablespoons)
1 teaspoon minced ginger
3 scallions (white and green parts),
   minced
1 tablespoon five-spice powder
   (see page 140)
¼ teaspoon sea salt
¼ cup Chinese rice wine (Shaoxing)
   or dry vermouth
2 tablespoons honey
2 tablespoons soy sauce
1 tablespoon sesame oil
2 pounds boneless, skinless chicken
   breasts or thighs, sliced across
   the grain into ⅛-inch strips
Six 18-inch squares aluminum foil
18 dried bamboo leaves, soaked in
   water for 30 minutes, dried, and
   trimmed to 9 inches in length
   (see page 39), or 24 dried corn
   husks, soaked in water for
   20 minutes, then dried
6 to 7 Napa cabbage leaves, torn
   into bite-sized pieces
½ lemon, thinly sliced
10 cilantro sprigs, coarsely
   chopped

Makes 6 servings

1. Combine garlic, ginger, scallions, five-spice powder, salt, wine, honey, soy sauce, and sesame oil in a large zippered plastic bag. Seal the bag and toss back and forth to mix. Add the chicken, seal, and toss the bag back and forth until the chicken pieces are well coated with the marinade. Refrigerate for at least 1 hour, or overnight.

2. Heat the grill.

3. While waiting for the grill to get hot, remove the chicken from the refrigerator. Line an aluminum foil square with 2 overlapping bamboo leaves. Place a few pieces of cabbage in the center of the leaves. Top with approximately ½ cup of chicken. Garnish with a lemon slice and a tablespoon of the cilantro. Cover with another bamboo leaf and fold the leaves into a square package. Wrap the aluminum foil around it to make a tight pouch. Repeat with the remaining ingredients.

4. Rake the hot coals into a mound on one side of the grill. Put the pouches on the rack directly over the hot coals. Grill for 5 minutes, occasionally flipping them carefully. Move the pouches to the empty side of the grill, cover, and grill-smoke for 15 minutes. Be sure to open the air vents in the top of the grill cover. Unwrap one of the pouches to check if the chicken is cooked: it should feel firm to touch and the juices should run clear when it is pierced with a knife. Transfer the pouches to a serving platter.

5. Unwrap and transfer the chicken to a platter. Discard the leaves and foil, and serve.

Myanmar-Style Grilled Duck

THIS IS A MYANMAR RECIPE from the country's indigenous Shan-Burmese people. The seasonings are similar to those used in southern Chinese cooking. Grill-smoking leaves the duck tender and moist, with a smoky aroma. Serve with steamed Thai long-grain jasmine rice (see page 105) and Burmese Cucumber Relish (page 153).

1. Put the Szechwan peppercorns in a small skillet and dry-roast over medium-high heat, sliding the skillet back and forth over the burner to prevent burning, until the peppercorns exude a pleasant aroma, about 1 minute. Remove from the heat, transfer to a bowl, and let cool. Repeat with the cumin seeds.

2. Grind the spices in a spice grinder and transfer to a zippered plastic bag. Add the garlic, ginger, five-spice powder, red pepper, salt, onion, tomato, orange, and vegetable oil. Seal the bag and toss gently back and forth. Add the duck breasts, seal, and toss until well coated. Refrigerate for at least 1 hour, or overnight.

3. Heat the grill.

4. While waiting for the grill to get hot, remove the duck from the refrigerator. Line an aluminum foil square with a banana leaf. Put a duck breast, with 2 tablespoons of the marinade, in the center of the banana leaf. Fold the leaf over the duck to make a square package. Wrap the aluminum foil around it to make a tight pouch. Repeat with the remaining duck.

5. Rake the hot coals into a mound on one side of the grill. Put the pouches on the rack directly over the hot coals. Grill for about 5 minutes, occasionally turning them carefully. Move the pouches to the empty side of the grill, cover, and grill-smoke for 12 minutes. Be sure to open the air vents in the top of the grill cover. Unseal one of the pouches to check if the duck is cooked: the outside should be done, but the inside still rare and pink. Transfer to a platter.

6. To serve, undo the pouches and transfer the duck and sauce to a serving platter.

1 tablespoon Szechwan peppercorns
1 tablespoon cumin seeds
4 garlic cloves, minced (2 tablespoons)
1 tablespoon minced ginger
1 tablespoon five-spice powder (see page 140)
1 tablespoon crushed red pepper
½ teaspoon sea salt
1 medium yellow onion, minced (¾ cup)
1 medium tomato, minced
1 small orange, with peel, seeded and pureed
1 tablespoon vegetable oil
6 boneless duck breasts, scored lightly
Six 12-inch squares aluminum foil
Six 8 × 10-inch pieces banana leaves (see page 38)

Makes 6 servings

Savory Mushrooms in Banana Leaves

IN THAILAND, wrapping food foraged from the forest or river in banana pouches, then grilling it, is called *nyop,* meaning to bury. To duplicate the taste of tropical mushrooms, use fresh oyster or shiitake mushrooms. Serve with steamed Thai long-grain jasmine rice (see page 105).

1 teaspoon white peppercorns

½ teaspoon sea salt

5 garlic cloves, minced
(2½ tablespoons)

5 cilantro stems with roots, minced

15 chiles de árbol, softened in hot
water, dried, half seeded, half not,
and minced

1 stalk lemongrass, tough outer layers
and green parts removed, minced

1 teaspoon minced galangal or ginger

Grated zest of 1 kaffir or regular lime

1 shallot, minced

1 teaspoon fermented shrimp paste
(or substitute red miso)

2 tablespoons grated coconut
(see page 135)

3 tablespoons fish sauce (nam pla)
(or substitute soy sauce for a
vegetarian dish)

1 teaspoon sugar

1 pound oyster mushrooms,
trimmed, or shiitake, stems
removed and sliced into
thin slices

Four 12-inch squares aluminum foil

Four 8 × 10-inch pieces banana leaves
(see page 38)

12 arugula sprigs

3 kaffir lime leaves, slivered, or
slivered zest of 1 lime

2 serrano chiles, seeded and slivered

Makes 4 servings

1. Put the peppercorns in a skillet and dry-roast over medium-high heat, sliding the skillet back and forth over the burner to prevent burning, until the peppercorns exude a pleasant aroma, about 1 minute. Remove from the heat and transfer to a bowl to cool. Grind in a spice grinder and set aside.

2. Pound the salt and garlic in a mortar with a pestle into a paste. One at a time, add the cilantro, peppercorns, chiles, lemongrass, galangal, lime zest, shallot, and shrimp paste, in sequence, adding each only after the previous ingredient has been pureed and incorporated. Transfer to a mixing bowl and add coconut flakes, fish sauce, and the sugar. Mix thoroughly. Add the mushrooms and mix well.

3. Heat the grill.

4. While waiting for the grill to get hot, line an aluminum foil square with a banana leaf. Put 3 arugula sprigs in the center and top with one-quarter of the mushrooms. Garnish with slivers of kaffir leaves and serrano chiles. Fold the banana leaf over the mixture to make a square package. Wrap the aluminum foil around the banana leaf to make a tight pouch. Repeat with the remaining ingredients.

5. Rake the hot coals into a mound on one side of the grill. Put the pouches on the rack directly over the hot coals. Grill, turning a couple of times, for about 5 minutes. Move the pouches to the empty side of the grill, cover, and grill-smoke for 10 minutes. Be sure to open the air vents in the top of the grill cover. Open one of the pouches to check: the mushrooms should be soft and tender. Transfer to a serving platter.

6. Unfold the pouches and serve.

Thai Quesadillas

QUESADILLAS, MEXICAN GRILLED CHEESE sandwiches made with flour or corn tortillas instead of bread, were a favorite food in my college years. I was living in a dormitory without a kitchen, and they were one of the few things I could make in my room. After filling the tortilla with whatever was on hand—leftover hamburger, chicken, even hot dogs—and adding plenty of chiles, I wrapped the whole thing in aluminum foil and "cooked" the package with a hot iron! Presto! I had a great meal. This is one of my favorite combinations.

1. Put the peppercorns in a small skillet and dry-roast over medium-high heat, sliding the skillet back and forth over the burner to prevent burning, until the peppercorns exude a pleasant aroma, about 1 minute. Remove from the heat and transfer to a bowl to cool. Repeat with the coriander seeds.

2. Grind the peppercorns and coriander seeds in a spice grinder. Transfer to a bowl and add the garlic, chiles, lemongrass, and salt. Mix well and set aside.

3. Heat the oil in a large skillet over high heat for 5 to 6 seconds, until hot. Add the seasoning mixture and stir-fry until it exudes a wonderful aroma, about 30 seconds. Add the chicken (or beef, shrimp, or mushrooms), and stir-fry until partially cooked. Add the fish sauce and stir-fry until the chicken is cooked, 1 to 2 minutes. Remove from the heat and set aside.

4. Heat the grill.

5. While waiting for the grill to get hot, combine the Cheddar and Muenster in a bowl. Spread a thin layer of the cheese over one half of a tortilla and top with a few slices of shallot, a couple of tomato slices, a few tablespoons of the filling mixture, and one-quarter of the basil leaves. Top with more cheese and fold the empty side of the tortilla over the filling. Repeat with the remaining ingredients.

6. Carefully put the quesadillas on the grill over low heat. Grill for 1 to 2 minutes, then carefully flip over with a spatula. Continue to flip and grill until the cheese is melted and the tortillas are crisp and lightly browned.

7. Transfer the quesadillas to a cutting board and cool for 1 to 2 minutes before slicing into wedges. Serve hot.

½ teaspoon white peppercorns
½ teaspoon coriander seeds
3 garlic cloves, minced
6 serrano chiles, seeded or not, depending on your preference for spiciness, and minced
1 stalk lemongrass, tough outer layers and green parts removed, minced
½ teaspoon sea salt
3 tablespoons olive oil
1 cup thinly sliced skinless, boneless chicken, beef, shrimp, or portobello mushroom caps
1 tablespoon fish sauce (nam pla)
1 cup grated Cheddar
1 cup grated Muenster
Four 9-inch flour tortillas
2 shallots, thinly sliced
1 small tomato, thinly sliced
½ cup Thai basil leaves

Makes 4 quesadillas

Grilled Marinated Catfish in Banana Leaves

THAI OLD-TIMERS, remembering happier moments in the past, speak fondly of the monsoon seasons when flooding rivers and canals were engorged with multitudes of tiny fish and shrimp. In those days, fish literally jumped from the water into waiting hands or buckets. When night fell, the fresh-caught fish, perhaps wrapped in banana leaves as in this dish, were cooked over a bonfire to celebrate.

Serve the catfish with steamed Thai long-grain jasmine rice (see page 105) and Chiles, Garlic, Fish Sauce, and Lime Juice (page 144).

1 teaspoon sea salt

6 garlic cloves, minced

15 chiles de árbol, softened in hot water dried, and minced

1 teaspoon minced cilantro stems with roots

1 stalk lemongrass, tough outer layers and green parts removed, minced

1 tablespoon minced galangal or ginger

1 teaspoon minced kaffir or regular lime zest

1 shallot, minced

1 teaspoon fermented shrimp paste or red miso

1 large egg, slightly beaten

2 tablespoons fish sauce (nam pla)

1 cup plus 6 tablespoon coconut cream (see page 135)

2 pounds catfish fillets, sliced into approximately ½ × 3-inch-long strips

Six 18-inch squares aluminum foil

Six 9 × 10-inch pieces banana leaves (see page 38)

1 small cabbage, leaves separated, parboiled until tender, drained, and thoroughly dried

3 to 4 Thai basil sprigs; leaves only

2 kaffir lime leaves, slivered, or slivered zest of 1 lime

2 red serrano chiles, seeded and slivered

Makes 6 servings

1. Using a mortar and pestle, pound the salt and garlic into a fine paste. One at a time, add the chiles, cilantro, lemongrass, galangal, minced lime zest, shallot, and shrimp paste, in sequence, adding each one only after the previous ingredient has been pureed and incorporated into the paste.

2. Transfer the paste to a mixing bowl. Add the beaten egg and fish sauce and mix well. Add 1 cup of the coconut cream and mix to combine. Add the catfish and stir to coat.

3. Heat the grill.

4. While waiting for the grill to get hot, line an aluminum foil square with a banana leaf. Stack a couple of cabbage leaves in the center of the banana leaf and top with about 1 cup of the fish mixture. Garnish with a tablespoon of the remaining coconut cream, a couple of basil leaves, several slivers of kaffir lime leaf, and some chile slivers. Fold the banana leaf over the filling to make a square package, and wrap it in the aluminum foil to make a tight pouch. Repeat with the remaining ingredients.

5. Rake the hot coals into a mound on one side of the grill. Put the pouches on the rack directly over the hot coals and grill for 5 minutes. Move the pouches to the empty side, cover and grill-smoke for about 9 minutes. Be sure to open the air vents in the top the grill cover. Open one of the pouches to check: the fish should be firm and white.

6. Transfer the pouches to a serving platter, open them, and serve.

Otak Otak Nonya-Style Spicy Fish Cakes

BECAUSE I WAS BROUGHT up eating dishes heavily seasoned with garlic, when I first tasted Malaysian food, I wasn't prepared to like it, since onions rather than garlic are predominate. I was wrong. These soft golden fish cakes are light, delicate, and delicious. Serve with Chayote Relish (page 155).

1. Combine the turmeric, chiles, almonds, galangal, onion, sugar, salt, and shrimp paste in a food processor and process for 1 minute. Add the egg and coconut cream and process to a smooth paste. Add the fish and process until the mixture turns into a paste and begins to form a ball. Transfer to a mixing bowl, add the kaffir lime leaves, and mix well. Set aside.

2. Heat the grill.

3. While waiting for the grill to get hot, line an aluminum foil square with a banana leaf. Put about 1 cup of the fish mixture in the center of the leaf and fold it into a square package. Wrap the aluminum foil around it to make a tight pouch. Repeat with the remaining ingredients.

4. Rake the hot coals into a mound on one side of the grill. Put the pouches on the rack directly over the coals and grill for 5 minutes. Move the pouches to the empty side, cover, and grill-smoke for about 8 minutes. Be sure to open the air vents in the top of the grill cover. Open one of the pouches to check if the fish is cooked: it should feel firm, and when pierced with a bamboo skewer, the skewer should come out clean.

5. Transfer the pouches to a serving platter, unwrap them, and serve.

One 1-inch chunk fresh turmeric, peeled and minced, or 1 teaspoon turmeric powder mixed with 1 tablespoon minced ginger

15 chiles de árbol, softened in hot water, dried, half seeded, half not, and minced

6 serrano chiles, seeded and minced

1 tablespoon ground blanched almonds

1 tablespoon minced galangal or ginger

1 yellow onion, minced

1 tablespoon sugar

1 teaspoon sea salt

1 teaspoon fermented shrimp paste or red miso

1 large egg, slightly beaten

1 cup coconut cream (see page 135)

2 pounds catfish fillets, cut into small chunks

4 kaffir lime leaves, slivered, or slivered zest of 1 lime

Six 12-inch squares aluminum foil

Six 9 × 10-inch pieces banana leaves (see page 38)

Makes 6 servings

Grilled Fish in Bamboo Leaves

THIS RECIPE IS REMINISCENT of my mother's steamed fish, heavy with the scents of ginger and sesame oil. Grilling makes the flesh firmer and infuses it with a smoky aroma.

1 teaspoon sugar

¼ teaspoon sea salt

½ cup rice vinegar

¼ cup soy sauce

2 tablespoons Chinese rice wine
(Shaoxing) or dry vermouth

1 teaspoon sesame oil

Two 18 × 20-inch pieces heavy-duty
aluminum foil

8 bamboo leaves, softened,
dried, and hard stems removed
(see page 39)

8 slices bacon

One 3-pound red snapper or sea
bass, cleaned and thoroughly
dried

12 thin slices ginger, slivered

3 scallions (white and green parts),
slivered

1 lemon, cut into 8 wedges

Makes 6 servings

1. Combine the sugar, salt, vinegar, soy sauce, wine, and sesame oil in a bowl. Mix well and set aside.

2. Heat the grill.

3. While waiting for the grill to get hot, line one aluminum foil sheet with 4 of the bamboo leaves and turn up the edges of the foil. Lay 4 slices of bacon lengthwise on top of the leaves.

4. Make 3 to 4 diagonal slashes into the meaty part of the fish on both sides and put it on top of the bacon. Fill the fish cavity with the ginger and scallions.

5. Pour the soy sauce mixture over the fish. Cover with the remaining 4 slices bacon, then cover with the remaining 4 bamboo leaves and the other sheet of foil. Roll the edges of the foil over to form a tight packet.

6. Carefully place the fish on the grill over medium heat. Cover and grill-smoke for 20 minutes. Be sure to open the air vents in the top of the grill cover. To check for doneness, carefully open the aluminum pouch: the flesh of the fish should be white and easily pierced with a bamboo skewer.

7. Transfer the fish to a serving platter, unwrap, and serve with the lemon wedges.

Feast from Chao Mae Kong Kha

ACCORDING TO LAOTIAN BELIEFS, the goddess Chao Mae Kong Kha rules the sea. She protects sea creatures and fishermen. This grand dish is named after her because it's not only spectacular to look at, but tastes absolutely heavenly—truly a gift from a goddess. Krachai, or Chinese keys, is a rhizome, sold preserved in brine or frozen, available in most Asian markets or through mail-order sources.

Serve it with either steamed Thai long-grain jasmine rice (see page 105) or sourdough bread and Chiles, Garlic, Fish Sauce, and Lime Juice (page 144).

1. Combine the salt, pepper, chiles, garlic, shallots, krachai, and kaffir lime leaves in a bowl and mix well. Add the seafood, basil leaves, arugula, and lemon slices. Toss to mix well.

2. Heat the grill.

3. While waiting for the grill to get hot, line an aluminum foil sheet with a banana leaf. Place the seafood mixture in the center of the leaf. Cover it with the second banana leaf and then the remaining aluminum foil. Roll the edges of the aluminum foil over tightly to form a pouch.

4. Put the pouch on the grill over medium-high heat. Cover and grill-smoke for 20 minutes. Be sure to open the air vents in the top of the grill cover. Carefully open the pouch slightly to make sure that the mussel shells are open and the lobster shell has turned pink. Remove the pouch from the grill and transfer the seafood, along with the juices, to a platter and serve.

1½ teaspoons sea salt

1 teaspoon freshly ground white pepper

6 to 7 fresh bird chiles or 5 serrano chiles, slivered

12 garlic cloves, thinly sliced

3 shallots, thinly sliced

12 slivers ginger or 4 krachai, thinly sliced

10 kaffir lime leaves torn in half, or slivered zest of 2 limes

1 pound large shrimp, peeled, deveined, and thoroughly dried

1 pound mussels, scrubbed, debearded, and thoroughly dried

1 pound clams, scrubbed and thoroughly dried

One 1½-pound lobster, chopped into bite-sized pieces

2 cups Thai basil leaves

2 cups arugula leaves, slightly torn into bite-sized pieces

1 lemon, thinly sliced

Two 18 × 23-inch pieces aluminum foil

Two 16 × 18-inch pieces banana leaves (see page 38)

Makes 8 to 10 servings

Grilled Fish in Sea Salt

THERE ARE SEVERAL VENDORS in provinces near the Gulf of Thailand who sell salt-encrusted grilled fish like these at weekend markets. Some vendors stuff the fish with sprigs of pandanus leaves or lemongrass before enclosing it in the pristine white sea salt. After grilling, the salt is chipped away, revealing a moist, juicy, aromatic fish.

Serve with steamed Thai long-grain jasmine rice (see page 105) and Chiles, Garlic, Fish Sauce, and Lime Juice (page 144).

One 2-pound red snapper or salmon, trout, or sea bass, cleaned
4 garlic cloves, bruised
4 to 6 fresh bird chiles or 3 to 4 serrano chiles, bruised
2 stalks lemongrass, tough outer layers removed, sliced into 4-inch lengths and bruised
2 to 3 toothpicks, soaked in water for 30 minutes, then dried
One 18-inch square heavy-duty aluminum foil
4 cups sea salt
½ cup egg whites (3 eggs)

Makes 4 servings

1. Rinse the fish and pat the cavity dry. Stuff the cavity with the garlic, chiles, and lemongrass. Secure the opening with the toothpicks.

2. Heat the grill.

3. While waiting for the grill to get hot, lay the foil on a cookie sheet. Combine the sea salt and egg whites in a bowl; the mixture should look like wet cornmeal. Spread the mixture over the aluminum foil. Put the fish on the salt mixture and pack it tightly over the fish.

4. Carefully pick up the foil holding the fish and place it on the grill over a medium-high heat. Cover and grill-smoke for 15 to 20 minutes. Be sure to open the air vents in the top of the grill cover. To test for doneness, insert a metal skewer into the thickest part of the fish: it should pierce through easily.

5. Transfer the fish to a cutting board. Remove the salt crust by tapping with a knife, then peel off the skin. Transfer the fish to a platter and serve.

Huroko-Style Scallops

IRON CHEF, the Japanese cooking series, has become wildly popular in the United States. On one show, one of the two competing chefs prepared Huroko-style grilled scallops in a covered earthenware dish. I duplicated it with some modifications. The scallops will taste as if freshly harvested from the sea, tender and light as a feather. Salmon roe (ikura) and seasoned capelin roe (koganekko masago) are available in the refrigerated sections of Japanese markets.

1. Combine the mirin, soy sauce, and ginger in a bowl. Mix well, then add the scallops. Cover and refrigerate for 30 minutes.

2. Heat the grill.

3. While waiting for the grill to get hot, crumble the tofu onto a piece of cheesecloth. Wrap the tofu in the cloth and squeeze out as much water as possible. Unwrap and put the tofu in the food processor. Add the sesame oil and pepper and process until the tofu resembles heavy cream, about 2 minutes. Transfer to a mixing bowl, and very gently fold in the salmon roe.

4. Remove the scallops from the refrigerator. Line one aluminum foil square with 2 crisscrossed bamboo leaves. Spoon a couple of tablespoons of the tofu mixture into the center and flatten it. Top with a scallop and a tablespoon of the marinade. Garnish with a lemon slice. Fold the bamboo leaves over the filling, making a square package, then wrap in the foil to make a tight pouch. Repeat with the remaining tofu and scallops.

5. Place the pouches on the grill over medium heat and grill for 3 minutes. Turn and grill until the scallops are cooked through, 3 to 4 minutes longer. Remove from the grill.

6. Unwrap the packages and transfer the scallops to a serving platter. Top each with a teaspoon of the capelin roe, and serve immediately with the pickled ginger.

⅓ cup mirin (sweet rice wine)
1 tablespoon soy sauce
3 tablespoons minced ginger
10 large sea scallops (about ½ pound)
One 16-ounce package tofu, drained
1 tablespoon sesame oil
¼ teaspoon freshly ground white pepper
2 tablespoons salmon roe (ikura)
Ten 12-inch squares aluminum foil
20 bamboo leaves, soaked and dried (see page 39)
10 thin lemon slices
¼ cup seasoned capelin roe (koganekko masago)
½ cup pickled ginger

Makes 10 packages

Grilled and Wrapped

BABOO, an Indian, was our neighborhood night watchman. We children were petrified of him. At dusk, he sauntered into our alley, wearing a thin white cotton wrap and trailing another that billowed like a kite. His long jet-black hair was oiled and pulled high on top of his head. Carrying a big wooden stick, Baboo marched up and down the street, and as darkness crept in, the whites of Baboo's eyes glowed like fireflies. Eventually, he pulled down a string cot and leaned it against a massive gate. He would belt out strange Indian melodies. Night after night, he serenaded us to sleep.

Long before anyone awoke in the morning, Baboo was gone from his post. The neighborhood women were the first to see him again, when they walked to the municipal water pump to bathe. There was Baboo at work on a gleaming metal table, slapping, stretching, and fanning bundles of oiled dough into thin transparent sheets. After he coiled the dough, which looked, oddly enough, like his hair neatly piled into a bun on top of his head, Baboo patted it between his palms, making small flat disks.

Cooked on a hot griddle, the steaming flatbread, or roti, wrapped in banana leaves, was bought by the freshly bathed women, carrying water buckets, to take home to their families for breakfast.

Walking by the shophouses in Baboo's neighborhood, we could smell the unfamiliar Indian spices the women used for cooking. Passing by Baboo's house one day, I saw him sitting on the cement floor in the middle of his dark room with a metal plate. He was tearing and using pieces of roti to pick up tiny morsels from his plate. Delighted with my discovery, I told my father what I had seen.

During his youth as a salesman in Southeast Asia, my father had often encountered Indian, Pakistani, and Persian immigrants in Singapore and Malaysia who ate flatbread similar to the kind my father's family made in northern China. In the Chinese version, scallions or garlic cloves are wrapped in the flatbread, and it is eaten alone or with other dishes. The Chinese do not use flatbread in place of utensils, nor do they eat with their hands. It would be considered extremely impolite, and, as Papa put it, "unsanitary and uncivilized."

Having been brought up among so many nationalities, I find that eating with one's hands is not only civilized but fun. When my mother made Shantung-style flatbread with scallions, I copied Baboo, tearing small pieces to scoop up chicken or stir-fried vegetables. This was the only time my parents, reluctantly, allowed me to eat with my hands.

Many of our Thai neighbors ate with their hands. Unlike the Indians, though, they did not use bread to wrap or scoop food. Instead they used rice, which was mixed with curry sauce, pieces of meat, or vegetables and pressed together. Laotians and Cambodians also eat this way. The Vietnamese are known for wrapping just about everything in fresh rice paper and lettuce leaves. It's an enjoyable way of eating, touching, and feeling the different textures of the food wrapped to suit your taste.

Wrapping food can turn an ordinary meal into a festive occasion. Watching crisp Vietnamese rice paper, after a bath in a bowl of very warm water, transform itself into soft, translucent sheets is magic.

Countless ingredients can be used to wrap grilled foods. The Mexican tortilla and Middle Eastern pita bread are probably the most familiar and common. But fresh (or frozen) flatbreads from India, such as chapati, roti, and naan are also used for this purpose. Lavash, large thin Middle Eastern sheet bread, is very popular, too. All are found in major supermarkets, as well as Middle Eastern and Indian markets. Asian markets also carry Chinese breads, from flatbreads with scallions to sesame pocket breads.

Fresh vegetables, including lettuce, bitter greens, and cabbages, make a simple wrap. I like to match crispy, sweet leaves with spicy grilled ingredients, or combine bitter leaves with something salty and spicy.

Vietnamese-Style Grilled Beef in Lettuce

MARINATED OVERNIGHT, the beef becomes tender, juicy, and perfumed by the spices. The grilled meat is served wrapped in rice paper with fresh vegetables and aromatic herbs. Serve with a double recipe of Vietnamese Sweet-and-Sour Sauce (page 149).

1. Combine the garlic, lemongrass, shallots, sugar, red pepper, salt, black pepper, sesame seeds, fish sauce, and sesame oil in a large zippered plastic bag. Seal and toss the bag back and forth to combine. Score the surface of the beef. Add the beef to the plastic bag, seal, and toss back and forth to coat. Refrigerate for at least 1 hour, or, for best results, overnight.

2. Heat the grill.

3. While waiting for the grill to get hot, remove the beef from the refrigerator.

4. Generously spray the beef with vegetable oil and put on the grill over medium-high heat. Grill, turning frequently to prevent burning, until the outer layer is brown. Spray with vegetable oil to keep the meat moist. Cover and grill until the beef is medium-rare, about 25 minutes. Be sure to open the air vents in the top of the grill cover. Transfer to a serving platter. Let sit for 5 minutes before slicing into long thin strips.

5. To serve, invite guests to bathe the rice paper, a sheet at a time, in a large bowl of very warm water. Shake off the excess water and lay the rice paper flat on the plate. When it is soft and pliable, line the center of the paper with a lettuce leaf. Top with 2 to 3 slices of beef, a few mint leaves, cilantro sprigs, and some sliced cucumber. Roll into a cylinder and dip in the sweet-and-sour sauce.

5 garlic cloves, minced
 (2½ tablespoons)
1 stalk lemongrass, tough outer
 layers and green parts removed,
 minced
3 shallots, minced
1 tablespoon sugar
1 tablespoon crushed red pepper
½ teaspoon sea salt
½ teaspoon freshly ground black
 pepper
1 tablespoon sesame seeds,
 toasted
2 tablespoons fish sauce (nam pla)
1 teaspoon sesame oil
2 pounds flank steak or tri-tip
Vegetable oil spray
Sixteen 9-inch-round rice papers
1 head red or green leaf lettuce,
 leaves separated, rinsed, and
 thoroughly dried
12 to 16 mint leaves
12 to 16 cilanto sprigs
1 cucumber, peeled, halved
 lengthwise, seeded, and thinly
 sliced lengthwise

Makes 6 to 8 servings

Korean-Style Grilled Beef in Lettuce

THE SUGAR in this marinade balances the saltiness of soy sauce, as well as caramelizing the meat. The beef is superb when wrapped in crisp, crunchy lettuce. Kimchi is a Korean spicy pickled cabbage, available in many supermarkets and Asian groceries. Serve with Grilled Potato, Egg, and Bean Thread Salad (page 91).

1. Combine the sugar, sake, minced garlic, green onion, soy sauce, sesame seeds, sesame oil, black pepper, and cayenne in a zippered plastic bag. Seal and toss the bag back and forth to combine. Add the meat and garlic cloves, seal, and toss the bag back and forth to coat the meat well. Refrigerate at least for 1 hour, or, for best results, overnight.

2. Heat the grill.

3. While waiting for the grill to get hot, remove the beef from the refrigerator. Transfer the beef, garlic cloves, and whole scallions to a platter. Drain the marinade into a bowl.

4. Place a fine-mesh grill rack on the regular rack. Spray the beef generously with the vegetable oil and place on the grill. Grill, basting with the reserved marinade and turning frequently to prevent burning, until medium-rare, about 8 minutes. Transfer to a serving platter and let sit for 5 minutes.

5. In the meantime, place the garlic cloves and scallions on the fine-mesh grill rack. Grill, turning frequently, until slightly charred and soft to the touch, about 2 minutes. Transfer to a serving platter and tent with aluminum foil to keep warm while you slice the beef.

6. Slice the beef into long thin pieces. Chop the green onions into bite-sized chunks. To eat, place 2 to 3 slices of meat, a clove of garlic, and 2 to 3 chunks of green onions on a lettuce leaf. Top with a pinch or two of kimchi and fold over the sides to make a complete bundle.

2 tablespoons sugar

⅓ cup sake or dry vermouth

28 garlic cloves, 8 minced, 20 peeled and left whole

14 scallions (green and white parts), 4 finely chopped, 10 left whole

½ cup soy sauce

1 tablespoon sesame seeds

1 tablespoon sesame oil

1 teaspoon freshly ground black pepper

1 teaspoon cayenne pepper

2 pounds top sirloin or flank steak

Vegetable oil spray

20 iceberg lettuce leaves

About 1 cup kimchi

Makes 6 to 8 servings

Grilled Curried Lamb Wrapped in Radicchio

THE BITTERNESS OF RADICCHIO reminds me of the wild bitter greens in Thailand that are used to wrap grilled meat. Pickled garlic can be bought in Asian markets.

2 tablespoons minced ginger
1 tablespoon Madras curry powder
1 tablespoon garam masala
    (see page 139)
2 star anise
1½ tablespoons sugar
1 teaspoon sea salt
¼ cup soy sauce
¼ cup sake or dry vermouth
1 tablespoon sesame seeds
2 pounds lean boneless leg of lamb
3 to 4 small leeks, halved
    lengthwise
Vegetable oil spray
12 radicchio leaves
12 cilantro sprigs
2 to 3 heads pickled garlic,
    separated into individual cloves,
    (or substitute 16 pickled pearl
    onions)
1 recipe Mint or Basil Mayonnaise
    (page 145)

Makes 6 to 8 servings

1. Combine the ginger, curry powder, garam masala, star anise, sugar, salt, soy sauce, sake, and sesame seeds in a large zippered plastic bag. Seal the bag and toss back and forth to combine. Set aside.

2. Starting from a longer side, slice horizontally through the middle of the lamb and open it out like a butterfly (or book). Make several slashes in the surface, then add to the plastic bag. Seal and toss the bag back and forth to coat. Refrigerate for at least 2 hours or, for best results, overnight.

3. Heat the grill.

4. While waiting for the grill to get hot, remove the lamb from the refrigerator. Transfer the lamb to a platter and drain the marinade into a bowl.

5. Rake the hot coals into a mound on one side of the grill. Spray the leeks with vegetable oil and place them directly on the coals. Grill, turning frequently, until the leeks are slightly charred and soft, about 5 minutes. Transfer to a platter and tent with aluminum foil to keep warm.

6. Spray the lamb generously with vegetable oil and put it on the grill directly over the hot coals. Grill, basting with the marinade and turning frequently, for 2 minutes. Move the lamb to the empty side of the grill, cover, and grill-smoke. Be sure to open the air vents in the top of the grill cover. Uncover and grill, basting the lamb with the reserved marinade every 7 minutes, until medium-rare, about 25 minutes in all. Transfer to a serving platter and let rest briefly.

7. Slice the lamb into long thin strips. Cut the leeks into bite-sized pieces. To eat, line a radicchio leaf with 2 to 3 slices of lamb and top with 2 to 3 pieces of leeks, a couple of pickled garlic cloves, and a tablespoon or more of the mayonnaise. Wrap and enjoy.

Grilled Chicken in
Chinese Flatbread with Scallions

MY MOTHER'S CHINESE FLATBREAD with scallions makes an excellent wrap for grilled chicken. Having been raised with spicy foods, I get my dose of chiles by spreading the flatbread with Tomato and Chile Sambal before topping it with the grilled chicken.

1. Put the peppercorns in a small skillet and dry-roast over medium-high heat, sliding the skillet back and forth over the burner to prevent burning, until the peppercorns exude a pleasant aroma, about 1 minute. Remove from the heat, transfer to a bowl, and let cool. Repeat with the coriander seeds. Grind the spices in a spice grinder.

2. Transfer the ground spices to a large zippered plastic bag. Add the garlic, minced cilantro, brown sugar, salt, soy sauce, sake, and sesame oil, seal, and toss the bag back and forth to combine. Add the chicken, seal, and toss to coat the chicken. Refrigerate for at least 1 hour or, for best results, overnight.

3. Heat the grill.

4. While waiting for the grill to get hot, remove the chicken from the refrigerator. Transfer the chicken to a platter and pour the marinade into a bowl.

5. Spray the chicken generously with vegetable oil and place on the grill over medium-high heat. Grill, turning frequently to prevent burning, and basting with the reserved marinade, until the meat is firm: 7 to 8 minutes for breasts, about 6 minutes for thighs. Transfer to a platter.

6. When it is cool enough to handle, slice the chicken into bite-sized pieces. Spread each flatbread with 1 to 2 tablespoons of the sambal, and top with a few chicken pieces and a sprig of cilantro. Wrap and enjoy.

1 tablespoon white peppercorns
1 tablespoon coriander seeds
6 garlic cloves, minced
    (3 tablespoons)
36 cilantro sprigs, 12 minced,
    24 left whole
1 tablespoon brown sugar
1 teaspoon sea salt
¼ cup soy sauce
¼ cup sake or dry vermouth
1 teaspoon sesame oil
2 pounds boneless, skinless chicken
    breasts or thighs
Vegetable oil spray
2 recipes, or 6 Chinese Flatbreads
    with Scallions, quartered
    (page 115)
1 recipe Tomato and Chile Sambal
    (page 146)

Makes 6 servings

Lao Sausage in Napa Cabbage Leaves with Ginger and Roasted Peanuts

LAO SAUSAGE IS AROMATIC with a light, peppery taste. Traditionally fatty meat is used, but I prefer leaner cuts, which are just as tasty. Making sausages is easy, especially if you do it with a team of good friends. If you prefer to buy the sausage, select spicy and sweet ones in the Italian or Portuguese style.

1. Grind the chiles to a powder in a spice grinder. Transfer to a food processor. Add all the remaining ingredients except the pork and sausage casing. Puree into a smooth paste and transfer to a bowl. Do not wash the food processor bowl.

2. Add one-quarter of the pork to the processor, and grind until it forms a ball. Add one-quarter of the seasoning paste and blend to mix. Transfer to a bowl and repeat with the remaining pork and seasoning mixture.

3. Carefully fit the opening of the casing onto the faucet and, holding it tightly, turn on the cold water and run water through the entire casing. Remove from the faucet, rinse, and pat dry. Cut the casing into six 13-inch lengths and tie one end of each one with twine.

4. Fit a pastry bag with a plastic coupler (no tip) and fill it with the sausage mixture. Twist the top of the bag to force the meat into the coupler and to eliminate air pockets. Carefully fit approximately 1 inch of a casing over the coupler. Holding on to the casing and coupler, squeeze the mixture into the casing until the sausage is approximately 1 inch in diameter. Remove the casing from the coupler and tie the end with twine. Twist the center of the sausage so that the long sausage link is divided into two equal links, and tie the center with twine. Repeat with the remaining sausage mixture and casing. Refrigerate until ready to use. It will keep for 2 to 3 days. Or place in a zippered plastic bag and freeze; it will keep for at least a month.

Sausages

Makes twelve 6-inch links

25 chiles de árbol, half seeded, half not
1 tablespoon sea salt
12 garlic cloves, minced (¼ cup)
2 stalks lemongrass, tough outer layers and green parts removed, minced
¼ cup minced galangal or ginger
Minced zest of 1 kaffir lime or 2 regular limes
½ cup minced cilantro stems with roots
3 shallots, minced
12 kaffir lime leaves, minced, or minced zest of 1 lime
2 tablespoons fish sauce (nam pla)
2½ pounds boneless pork loin, cut into 1-inch chunks
About 1 ounce sausage casing
Thirty-six 12-inch lengths kitchen twine

• • •

3 to 4 Lao Pork Sausages

24 cilantro sprigs

12 thin slices young ginger
(see Note)

½ cup unsalted dry-roasted
peanuts

12 napa cabbage leaves

Makes 6 servings

5. Heat the grill.

6. Place the sausages on the grill over medium-low heat. Grill, turning occasionally, until slightly charred and the juices run clear when a sausage is pierced with a knife, approximately 12 minutes. Transfer to a serving platter.

7. When the sausages are cool enough to handle, cut into thin diagonal slices.

8. Wrap 2 to 3 slices of sausage, a sprig or two of cilantro, a slice of ginger, and several peanuts in each cabbage leaf. Enjoy.

Variation: The sausages can be made without the casing. Put 3 tablespoons of the mixture in the center of a 12-inch square of plastic wrap. Roll up into a cylinder. Squeeze both ends to tighten the roll and eliminate any air pockets, then tie each end with twine. Steam the sausages in boiling water for 2 minutes. Cool before unwrapping, then grill over medium-high heat for 3 to 5 minutes.

Note: If young ginger is unavailable, substitute 12 slices mature ginger. Massage it with 1 tablespoon sea salt, leave to sit for 15 minutes, then rinse and dry.

Spicy Meat Patties and Raita in Tortillas

ONE SUMMER, MY COMPANION Italo and I visited Vail, Colorado, where he had an art exhibition. While he was busy, I explored the neighborhood around the gallery and found a street vendor selling this wrap. Pickled ginger is available in Asian markets and many supermarkets.

1. Heat the grill.

2. While waiting for the grill to get hot, heat the oil in a small skillet over high heat for 5 seconds. Add the mustard seeds, cover the skillet to prevent the seeds from popping out, and heat, sliding the skillet back and forth over the burner to ensure even frying, for 30 seconds. Remove from the heat and let cool.

3. Combine the meat, mustard seeds, chopped onion, garlic, minced cilantro, ginger, garam masala, cayenne, salt, and turmeric powder in a bowl and mix well. Scoop up a handful of meat and form it into a 2 × 4-inch cylindrical patty, flattening it slightly. Repeat with the remaining meat.

4. Generously spray a fine-mesh grill rack with vegetable oil and put it on top of the regular rack. Baste the patties with yogurt and put them on the grill over medium-high heat. Grill, continuing to baste with the yogurt and turning frequently to prevent burning, until slightly charred and cooked through, about 8 to 9 minutes. Transfer to a platter and tent with aluminum foil to keep warm.

5. One at a time, warm the tortillas on the grill for 1 to 2 minutes. Transfer to a work surface. While hot, line with lettuce. Top each with 1 to 2 slices of tomato and 4 to 5 onion slices. Break the patties into bite-sized pieces and add a few pieces to the filling. Spoon the raita over the meat and top with 1 to 2 slices of jalapeño chile, if using, a cilantro sprig, and a couple of slices of pickled ginger. Starting from the side closest to you, fold the tortilla partway over the filling, then fold the opposite side over. From left to right, roll the tortilla up into a tight cylinder. Repeat with the remaining tortillas. Cut each wrap in half, and serve with the remaining raita.

1 tablespoon vegetable oil
1 teaspoon mustard seeds
1 pound ground beef or lamb
2 medium onions, 1 finely chopped, 1 thinly sliced
4 garlic cloves, minced
½ cup cilantro leaves, minced, plus 8 sprigs
2 tablespoons minced ginger
1 tablespoon garam masala (see page 139)
1 tablespoon cayenne pepper
1 teaspoon sea salt
1 teaspoon turmeric powder
Vegetable oil spray
½ cup plain yogurt
Eight 9-inch flour tortillas
4 to 5 iceberg lettuce leaves, torn into bite-sized pieces
1 small tomato, thinly sliced
1 to 2 jalapeño chiles, slivered (optional)
¼ cup pickled ginger
1 recipe Raita (page 150)

Makes 6 servings

Grilled Shrimp in Rice Paper

IN THIS THAI-VIETNAMESE wrap, the Vietnamese preference for sweet flavors is balanced with the hot and spicy flavors of Thai cooking.

5 garlic cloves, minced
    (2½ tablespoons)
2 shallots, minced
1 tablespoon sugar
¼ teaspoon sea salt
½ teaspoon freshly ground black
    pepper
20 mint leaves, 8 minced, 12 left
    whole
Minced zest of 1 lemon
2 tablespoons fish sauce (nam pla)
1 tablespoon olive oil
1½ pounds large shrimp, peeled,
    deveined, and thoroughly dried
Vegetable oil spray
Twelve 9-inch round rice papers
7 red or green leaf lettuce leaves,
    torn into bite-sized pieces
1 cucumber, peeled, halved
    lengthwise, seeded, and thinly
    sliced lengthwise
12 cilantro sprigs
1 to 2 jalapeño chiles, slivered
1 recipe Vietnamese Sweet-and-
    Sour Sauce (page 149)

Makes 12 wraps

1. Heat the grill.

2. While waiting for the grill to get hot, combine the garlic, shallots, sugar, salt, pepper, minced mint, lemon zest, fish sauce, and oil in a medium bowl. Mix well. Add the shrimp and toss to mix. Cover and refrigerate for 20 minutes.

3. Place a fine-mesh grill rack on top of the regular rack. Remove the shrimp from the refrigerator. Generously spray the shrimp with vegetable oil and place on the grill over medium-high heat. Grill, turning occasionally to prevent burning, until the shrimp are slightly charred, pink, and firm, 3 to 4 minutes. Transfer to a platter.

4. Bathe a rice paper in a bowl of very warm water. Shake off the excess water and lay it flat on a work surface. Line with several pieces of lettuce and top with 2 to 3 cucumber slices, 3 to 4 shrimp, a mint leaf, a cilantro sprig, and a couple of slivers of chile. Fold the bottom edge of the rice paper over the filling. From left to right, fold the rice paper over the filling and roll up into a cylinder. Repeat with the remaining ingredients. Serve with the sweet-and-sour sauce.

Grilled Vegetables in Rice Paper

WHEN I VISITED MY daughter, Angela, several years ago while she was living in Paris, her friends begged me to cook for them. There was a Vietnamese market near the apartment where I found rice papers. The fresh vegetables came from the neighborhood open-air market.

2 garlic cloves, minced

2 serrano chiles, minced

1 teaspoon sea salt

½ teaspoon freshly ground white pepper

Grated zest and juice of 1 orange

3 tablespoons soy sauce

1 tablespoon olive oil

1 red bell pepper

Vegetable oil spray

12 stalks asparagus

2 Japanese eggplants, hard stem ends removed

2 zucchini, quartered lengthwise

1 portobello mushroom, stem removed

2 ounces thin rice noodles or rice sticks

Twelve 9-inch round rice papers

7 red or green leaf lettuce leaves, torn into bite-sized pieces

24 mint leaves

12 cilantro sprigs

1 recipe Vietnamese Sweet-and-Sour Sauce with Tamarind Juice (page 149)

Makes 12 wraps

1. To make the seasoning mixture, combine the garlic, chiles, salt, pepper, orange zest and juice, soy sauce, and olive oil in a bowl. Set aside.

2. Heat the grill.

3. Place the red bell pepper on the grill over high heat and grill until the skin is completely charred, 7 to 8 minutes. Place in a paper bag, close tightly, and let sit until cool. Remove and rinse under cool water to peel off the outer charred skin. Pat dry, slice into long thin strips, and put in a large bowl.

4. Meanwhile, generously spray the asparagus, eggplant, zucchini, and mushroom with vegetable oil. Place on the grill over medium heat and grill the asparagus until the color brightens and they are slightly charred, approximately 3 minutes; cook the eggplants until soft, for 5 to 6 minutes; and the zucchini and mushroom until tender, 6 to 7 minutes. Transfer to the bowl with the bell pepper. Pour the seasoning mixture over the vegetables, toss lightly, and let sit for 15 minutes.

5. Slice the vegetables (except the bell pepper) into long thin strips, and set aside.

6. Cook the rice noodles in boiling water for 2 to 3 minutes, or until softened. Rinse several times under cool water. Squeeze the noodles, a handful at a time, to extract all the excess water, and dry thoroughly. Put in a bowl and set aside.

7. To assemble the wraps, bathe a rice paper in a bowl of very warm water. Shake off the excess water and place on a work surface. Line the rice paper with a couple of pieces of lettuce and top with a couple of tablespoons of rice noodles, a couple of strips each of red bell pepper, asparagus, eggplant, zucchini, and mushroom, 1 or 2 mint leaves, and a sprig of cilantro. Fold the bottom edge of the rice paper over the filling. From left to right, fold the rice paper over the filling and roll up into a cylinder. Repeat with the remaining ingredients. Serve the wraps with the sweet-and-sour sauce.

Grilled Scallops with Pineapple-Chile Glaze in Endive

MY COUSIN SUSIE is the "Pineapple Queen" of Thailand. Her company produces canned pineapple in a fiercely competitive market. She asked me to come up with ways of cooking with pineapple to promote her product. Susie and I love to eat this dish, which can be made with canned or fresh pineapple.

1. Heat the grill.

2. While waiting for the grill to get hot, combine the pineapple, ginger, chiles, honey, fish sauce, and salt in a small saucepan and cook over low heat, stirring frequently, for 5 minutes. Remove from the heat when the sauce is slightly thickened. Transfer to a bowl and let cool completely.

3. Add the lemon juice to the pineapple mixture, mixing well. Add the scallops, onion, and kumquats, and toss gently. Refrigerate for 30 minutes, but no more than 1 hour.

4. Remove the scallops from the refrigerator. Spray a fine-mesh grill rack with vegetable oil and put it on top of the regular rack. Spread the onion slices and kumquats on the rack over medium-high heat. Grill, turning frequently, until the onion turns translucent and the kumquats have softened, about 7 minutes. Transfer to a plate and tent with aluminum foil to keep warm.

5. Spray the scallops with vegetable oil and grill, turning occasionally, until slightly charred and firm, 5 to 6 minutes. Transfer to a plate.

6. To assemble, put several slices of onion and kumquat into each endive leaf. Top with a scallop. Dribble a teaspoon of mayonnaise on top and garnish with a caper. Serve hot.

1 cup chopped fresh or canned pineapple

1 tablespoon minced ginger

2 serrano chiles, minced

¼ cup honey

2 tablespoons fish sauce (nam pla)

¼ teaspoon sea salt

Juice of 1 lemon

1 pound large sea scallops

1 medium onion, thinly sliced

10 kumquats, thinly sliced and seeded

Vegetable oil spray

3 endive, larger leaves removed, smaller leaves reserved for another use

½ cup Mint Mayonnaise (page 145)

About ¼ cup salt-packed capers, rinsed and thoroughly dried

Makes 6 servings

Grilled Salads

GLITTERING nuggets of caramelized grilled meat bedded in a nest of bitter greens, the sharp tangy scent of a citrus vinaigrette mingled with smoky, earthy aromas: this is the epitome of an Asian grilled salad. Contrasting crisp but chewy grilled ingredients with soft and/or crunchy fruits and vegetables, Asian grilled salads are an unanticipated delight. They can also be made serendipitously, leaving room for individual expression.

By following these simple guidelines, you can create an Asian grilled salad at a moment's notice, and with great flair. The result will be so good that the only problem will be to remember how to duplicate it.

Flavors and Textures

Most Asian-style salads are packed with surprising flavors and textures. This is because they are served as an entrée with rice. Therefore, it's nice to use two or three kinds of meat, poultry, and/or seafood with various fresh vegetables or fruits. This will result in a bountiful salad. For a lighter variation, use just one kind of meat, poultry, or seafood.

If the flavor of the grilled ingredient is robust, match it with vegetables and fruits that are crisp, crunchy, and refreshing. For grilled seafood, use tangy-sweet flavored fruit and bitter greens.

Aromas

The smoky, toasty scents and flavors of the grilled ingredients add depth and provide contrast to fresh vegetables, fruits, and herbs. Perfume the salad with fresh herbs such as lemongrass, ginger, mint, cilantro, and basil, or other wild herbs. These add alluring scents and a light, refreshing balance to the grilled ingredients.

Dressing

Since the dressing should balance the ingredients, select a sharp-tasting dressing that's salty-sweet-sour and slightly spicy. Most of the time, dressings are made with combinations of salt, soy or fish sauce, sugar, vinegar, and/or fruit juice. Asian dressings tend to be very light because very little oil—or none—is included. When it is used, either olive or peanut oil is best for making vinaigrette dressings. For Japanese-, Korean-, or Chinese-style salads, use sesame oil for aroma. Ground peanuts add a distinctive and creamy flavor to Indonesian dressings.

Final Touches

In the West, garnishes often serve as decoration and are usually not eaten. In Asian salads, they are important ingredients.

After a salad is tossed with dressing, it's garnished with ingredients that provide contrasting and surprising textures, such as crunchy or crispy peanuts, garlic, or shallots.

Grilled Banana Blossom and Chicken Salad

THAI, LAOTIAN, CAMBODIAN, MYANMAR (Burmese), and Vietnamese cuisines all use raw banana blossoms for salads. This Thai recipe is unique because the banana blossoms are grilled, making them similar in texture and taste to grilled mushrooms. Banana blossoms are available in Asian markets. However, you can substitute portobello mushrooms or endive.

1. To make the crispy garlic, heat the oil in a small skillet over medium-high heat for 1 minute. Add the chopped garlic, stir, and add a couple of pinches of salt. Stir-fry until the garlic is golden, 4 to 5 minutes. Remove with a fine-mesh strainer to a plate lined with paper towels. Set aside to cool.

2. Heat the grill.

3. While waiting for the grill to get hot, combine the sugar, red pepper, ½ teaspoon of the salt, the fish sauce, and 2 tablespoons of the lime juice in a small bowl. Mix well and set aside.

4. Spray the head of the garlic and the shallot with vegetable oil, and place on the grill over medium-high heat. Grill, turning frequently, until the outer layers are slightly charred, about 15 minutes. Remove from the grill and let cool. Meanwhile, grill the banana blossoms over medium heat, turning frequently, until the outside petals are blackened, about 20 minutes. Remove from the grill and let cool.

5. Salt the chicken with the remaining ½ teaspoon of salt and generously spray with vegetable oil. Place on the grill and grill over medium-high heat, turning frequently to prevent burning, until the juices run clear when pierced with a fork, about 12 minutes. Transfer to a plate and let cool.

6. Slice the chicken into long thin pieces. Put in a bowl.

1 cup vegetable oil
¼ cup coarsely chopped garlic, plus 1 head garlic, top sliced off
2 tablespoons sugar
1 tablespoon crushed red pepper
1 teaspoon sea salt, plus a couple of pinches
2 tablespoons fish sauce (nam pla)
3 tablespoons fresh lime juice
1 shallot, not peeled
Vegetable oil spray
2 banana blossoms (or substitute 4 endive or 2 portobello mushrooms)
1 pound boneless, skinless chicken breasts
¼ cup coconut cream (see page 135)
9 mint leaves, torn and bruised
¼ cup unsalted dry-roasted peanuts, coarsely chopped

Makes 6 servings

7. Squeeze the soft garlic from the skin and add to the dressing. Peel and mince the shallot, then add to the dressing. Mix well.

8. Warm the coconut cream in a saucepan over low heat for 1 to 2 minutes. Add to the dressing and mix well.

9. Slice the banana blossoms lengthwise. Peel and discard the 5 to 6 outer petals to expose the soft inner petals. Discard the stamens (they resemble tiny bananas). Gather up the petals and slice crosswise into thin slivers. Mix with the remaining 1 tablespoon lime juice, then add to the chicken and toss lightly.

10. Add the dressing and mint leaves, and toss again. Transfer to a serving platter and garnish with the peanuts and crispy garlic.

11. If using endive, slice across the bulbs in long strands. For portobello mushrooms, slice into long strands.

Grilled Hamburger Salad

WHO NEEDS A BUN? In this recipe, the all-American hamburger is turned into an Asian grilled salad. There's no ketchup or mustard, but the rest of the typical garnishes—lettuce, tomato, and onion—are tossed together with the grilled meat, along with soft ripened fruit, such as peaches, apricots, or pears. You choose. Hamburger will never be the same.

Dressing

Makes about ½ cup

2 garlic cloves, minced
   (1 tablespoon)
1 teaspoon sea salt
3 tablespoons sugar
1 tablespoon fish sauce (nam pla)
¼ cup fresh lemon juice
1 tablespoon balsamic vinegar
1 teaspoon crushed red pepper

• • •

1 pound ground top sirloin
2 garlic cloves, minced
   (1 tablespoon)
1 teaspoon sea salt
1 teaspoon freshly ground white
   pepper
¼ cup finely chopped flat-leaf
   parsley
1 small onion, thinly sliced
1 cup cherry tomatoes, halved
½ cup thinly sliced radishes
¼ cup dried celery
4 to 5 romaine lettuce leaves, torn
   into bite-sized pieces
15 mint leaves, torn and bruised
Vegetable oil spray
¼ cup unsalted dry-roasted
   peanuts, coarsely chopped

Makes 6 servings

Make the Dressing

1. Combine all the ingredients in a mixing bowl. Set aside.

Make the Salad

2. Heat the grill.

3. While waiting for the grill to get hot, mix the beef, garlic, salt, pepper, and parsley in a mixing bowl. Shape into 6 patties, each approximately ½ inch thick and 2½ inches in diameter.

4. Combine the onion, cherry tomatoes, radishes, celery, lettuce, and mint leaves in a bowl. Toss gently; cover with a wet towel and refrigerate.

5. Spray the patties generously with vegetable oil and place on the grill over medium-high heat. After 1 to 2 minutes, flip the hamburgers. Grill, turning occasionally, until the juices run clear and the meat is cooked through, about 9 minutes. Transfer to a plate.

6. Remove the vegetables from the refrigerator. When the hamburgers are just cool enough to handle, break into bite-sized chunks and add to the vegetables. Pour on the dressing and toss. Transfer to a serving platter and garnish with the peanuts.

Grilled Lemongrass Chicken Salad

SEVERAL RECIPES IN THIS BOOK use only the hard bulb of lemongrass for seasoning pastes. The mild and tender green part, which is often discarded, is perfect for this salad. The slightly citrus flavor and perfume of lemongrass complements the chicken in this salad.

Make the Dressing

1. Combine all the ingredients in a bowl. Set aside.

Make the Salad

2. Heat the grill.

3. While waiting for the grill to get hot, slice the lemongrass on the diagonal into paper-thin slices. Separate into individual rings and put in a mixing bowl. Thinly slice the endive crosswise. Add to the bowl and set aside.

4. Put the sesame seeds in a small skillet and dry-roast over medium-high heat, sliding the skillet back and forth over the burner to prevent burning, until the seeds turn golden, 1 to 2 minutes. Remove from heat and transfer in a bowl to cool. Set aside.

5. Thread the garlic cloves onto the bamboo skewer, spray with vegetable oil, and place on the grill over medium-high heat. Rub the chicken breasts with the salt and spray generously with vegetable oil; put on the grill. Grill, turning frequently to prevent burning, until the garlic is slightly charred, about 4 minutes. When the chicken is pierced with a fork, the juices should run clear, about 9 minutes. Transfer to a plate.

6. When it is cool enough to handle, remove the garlic from the skewer, slice the cloves in half, and add to the bowl with the lemongrass. Slice the chicken diagonally into long thin strips. Add to the bowl.

7. Add the orange slices and sesame seeds, then add the dressing, toss lightly, and transfer to a serving platter.

Dressing

Makes ⅔ cup

1 tablespoon crushed red pepper
3 tablespoons fish sauce (nam pla)
¼ cup sugar
2 tablespoons fresh lime juice
¼ cup fresh orange juice

• • •

2 stalks lemongrass, tough outer layers and white parts removed; use only the tender green midsections
2 endives
¼ cup sesame seeds
7 garlic cloves
1 bamboo skewer, soaked in water for 30 minutes, then dried
1 pound boneless, skinless chicken breasts
½ teaspoon sea salt
Vegetable oil spray
1 orange, peeled and sectioned, membranes removed

Makes 6 servings

Grilled Duck, Pineapple, and Bitter Greens Salad

THIS IS ONE WAY of using leftover duck. However, the salad is so good that I often grill duck to make it.

Dressing

Makes ¼ cup

2 tablespoons sugar
1 tablespoon crushed red pepper
½ teaspoon sea salt
2 tablespoons fish sauce (nam pla)
2 tablespoons fresh lime juice

• • •

4 garlic cloves, minced
   (2 tablespoons)
2 tablespoons minced ginger
1 small onion, finely diced
1 jalapeño chile, minced
¼ cup balsamic vinegar
1 tablespoon hoisin sauce
1 tablespoon brown sugar
1 teaspoon sea salt
1½ pounds boneless duck breasts
1 cup fresh pineapple chunks
½ teaspoon freshly ground
   white pepper
2 to 3 bamboo skewers, soaked in
   water for 30 minutes, then dried
Vegetable oil spray
2 cups bitter greens, such as
   arugula or watercress, torn into
   bite-sized pieces
1 cup thinly sliced fennel

Makes 6 servings

Make the Dressing

1. Combine all the ingredients in a bowl, and set aside.

Make the Salad

2. Combine the garlic, ginger, onion, jalapeño chile, vinegar, hoisin sauce, sugar, and salt. Mix well, and transfer to a large zippered plastic bag. Add the duck, seal, and toss lightly to coat the duck. Refrigerate for at least 1 hour or, for best results, overnight.

3. Heat the grill.

4. While waiting for the grill to get hot, remove the duck from the refrigerator.

5. Rub the pineapple chunks with the pepper, and thread them onto the bamboo skewers. Spray with vegetable oil and place on the grill over medium-heat. Grill, turning frequently to prevent burning, until the pineapple is slightly charred, about 15 minutes. Transfer to a plate to cool. Remove the pineapple from the skewers, slice each chunk in half, and put in a bowl. Cover and set aside.

6. Meanwhile, remove the duck from the marinade and spray with vegetable oil. Put over medium heat and grill, turning frequently, until the skin is slightly charred, and medium-rare, 8 to 9 minutes. Transfer to a plate to cool.

7. Remove and discard the skin and slice the duck into long thin strips. Add to the bowl with the pineapple. Add the bitter greens and fennel, and toss lightly to mix. Add the dressing and toss gently once again. Transfer to a serving platter.

Vietnamese Grilled Beef with Green Mango Salad

AT A WORKSHOP on Southeast Asian foods held at the Culinary Institute of America in Napa, California, I watched two Vietnamese chefs make this salad. The crunchy, slightly sour green mango complements the smoky, caramelized grilled beef.

Make the Dressing

1. Combine all the ingredients in a saucepan and cook over medium-low heat until the salt and sugar are dissolved. Remove from the heat and let cool.

Make the Salad

2. Combine the lemongrass, shallots, garlic, sugar, pepper, soy sauce, fish sauce, and oil in a large zippered plastic bag. Seal and toss the bag back and forth to mix. Add the beef, seal, and toss gently back and forth to coat the beef. Refrigerate for at least 1 hour, but no more than 3 hours.

3. Put the sesame seeds in a small skillet and dry-roast over medium-high heat, sliding the skillet back and forth over the burner to prevent burning, until the seeds turn golden, 1 to 2 minutes. Remove from heat and transfer to a bowl to cool. Set aside.

4. Mound the charcoal in one side of the grill, leaving the other side empty. Heat the grill.

5. While waiting for the grill to get hot, spread the mango shreds on a platter; set aside. Remove the beef from the refrigerator. Drain the marinade into a bowl and set aside. Transfer the beef to a bowl and add the sesame seeds. Toss to coat. Thread 3 to 4 pieces of beef onto each bamboo skewer, in a tight bundle. Repeat with the remaining beef.

Dressing

Makes ⅓ cup

¼ teaspoon sea salt
2 fresh bird chiles or 1 red serrano chile, minced
1 teaspoon cayenne pepper
2 tablespoons sugar
2 tablespoons fish sauce (nam pla)
½ cup water

• • •

2 stalks lemongrass, tough outer layers and green parts removed, minced (½ cup)
2 shallots, minced (¼ cup)
2 garlic cloves, minced
3 tablespoons sugar
1 teaspoon freshly ground black pepper
3 tablespoons soy sauce
1 tablespoon fish sauce (nam pla)
1 tablespoon vegetable oil

1 pound top sirloin beef, thinly
   sliced on the diagonal against
   the grain
¼ cup sesame seeds
1 to 2 green mangoes, peeled,
   pitted, and shredded (2½ cups)
10 bamboo skewers, soaked in
   water for 30 minutes, then dried
Vegetable oil spray
20 mint leaves, torn and bruised

Makes 6 servings

6. Generously spray the beef with vegetable oil and place it on the grill directly over the hot coals, arranging the skewers close to one another. (The uncovered portion of the skewers should not be over the coals.) Grill, basting with the reserved marinade and turning frequently, 5 to 6 minutes for medium-rare beef, 7 to 8 minutes for well-done. Transfer the beef to a plate.

7. When it is just cool enough to handle, remove the beef from the skewers and add to the platter with the mango. Add the dressing and toss. Add the mint leaves; toss gently and serve.

Variation: Unpeeled Granny Smith apples can be substituted for the mangoes.

Indonesian-Style Grilled Vegetables with Peanut Dressing

THIS IS ONE OF those rare salads that can be made well ahead. The vegetables will keep beautifully for hours after grilling. The dressing can be made the day before; don't add the lime juice until just before serving. Store both the grilled vegetables and dressing in the refrigerator, and bring to room temperature before serving.

Make the Dressing

1. Place all the ingredients except the peanuts and lime juice in a food processor and puree.

2. Transfer to a saucepan and add the peanuts. Bring to a boil over high heat. Remove and let cool, then add the lime juice. Set aside.

Make the Vegetables

3. Heat the grill.

4. While waiting for the grill to get hot, combine the salt, cayenne, and oil in a large bowl. Mix well. Add all the vegetables, except the red bell pepper, and toss to coat. Set aside.

5. Place the red bell pepper on the hot grill and grill, turning occasionally, until completely charred, about 15 minutes. Transfer to a paper bag and seal. Let sit until cool enough to handle.

6. Rub the bag against the pepper inside to loosen the charred skin. Remove the pepper from the bag, rinse, and slice lengthwise in half. Rinse again to remove the seeds. Dry thoroughly, then slice into long thin strands. Put in a bowl and set aside.

Dressing

Makes ¾ cup

3 garlic cloves, minced
    (1½ tablespoons)
3 fresh bird chiles or 2 serrano
    chiles, minced
1 tablespoon minced ginger
2 tablespoons light brown sugar
2 tablespoons soy sauce
½ teaspoon freshly ground black
    pepper
½ cup water
½ cup unsalted dry-roasted
    peanuts, ground
2 tablespoons fresh lime juice

• • •

2 teaspoons sea salt

2 teaspoons cayenne pepper

¼ cup vegetable oil

1 medium onion, quartered

2 zucchini, halved lengthwise

1 portobello mushroom, stem
  removed

4 cups broccoli spears

1 cup green beans

2 cups asparagus, hard stem ends
  removed

1 red bell pepper

Grated zest of 2 lemons

Makes 6 servings

7. Meanwhile, place a fine-mesh grill rack directly on top of the regular rack. Place the onion, zucchini, mushroom, and broccoli on it, and grill over medium-high heat, turning frequently, until slightly charred and the insides are tender, 10 to 12 minutes. Transfer to a plate. Place the green beans and asparagus over medium heat and grill, turning until slightly charred, 3 to 4 minutes. Transfer to a plate with the other grilled vegetables.

8. When the vegetables are cool enough to handle, cut them into bite-sized pieces and add to the bowl with the pepper. Add the lemon zest and dressing. Mix well, and transfer to a serving platter.

Thai-Style Grilled Eggplant Salad

I OFTEN MAKE THIS quick and easy recipe for dinner after a busy day. Left-overs keep well overnight and can be tossed with pasta.

Make the Dressing

1. Combine the sugar, red pepper, salt, garlic, and fish sauce in a small saucepan and heat over medium heat until the sugar and salt are dissolved. Remove from the heat and let cool. Add the lime juice and set aside.

Make the Salad

2. Heat the grill.

3. While waiting for the grill to get hot, heat the oil in a small saucepan over high heat for a minute. Add the garlic and salt. Cook, stirring frequently to prevent burning, until the garlic is golden. With a fine-mesh strainer, transfer the garlic to a plate lined with paper towels; set aside. Transfer the oil to a heatproof container.

4. Score the flesh of the eggplants and generously brush with the garlic oil. Place on the grill over medium heat and grill, turning frequently to prevent burning, until the outside is slightly charred and the inside is soft when pierced with a fork, 6 to 7 minutes. Transfer to a plate.

5. When the eggplant is cool enough to handle, cut into bite-sized strands. Put in a bowl and add the shallots. Toss lightly, add the dressing, and mix well.

6. Add the mint and basil to the eggplant. Mix well. Transfer to a serving bowl and garnish with the crispy garlic.

Dressing

Makes ¼ cup

1 tablespoon sugar
1 tablespoon crushed red pepper
½ teaspoon sea salt
1 garlic clove, minced
2 tablespoons fish sauce (nam pla)
Juice of 1 lime

• • •

1 cup vegetable oil
5 garlic cloves, coarsely chopped
⅛ teaspoon sea salt
6 large Japanese eggplants, halved lengthwise
2 shallots, thinly sliced
10 mint leaves, torn and bruised
10 Thai basil leaves, torn and bruised

Makes 6 servings

Grilled Potato, Egg, and Bean Thread Salad

ONE OF THE UNIQUE sights for visitors to Asia are the vendors in northern Thailand, Laos, and Myanmar (Burma), who sell little round hen eggs grilled on portable charcoal grills. Grilled eggs have a smoky aroma. Both the eggs and potatoes are grilled for this salad, which goes well with Bulgogi—Korean Barbecued Beef (page 26).

Dressing

Makes ¾ cup

¼ teaspoon cumin seeds
3 tablespoons vegetable oil
1 medium onion, thinly sliced
3 tablespoons sugar
1 teaspoon cayenne pepper
½ teaspoon sea salt
3 tablespoons fish sauce (nam pla)
1 tablespoon fresh lime juice

• • •

4 ounces bean threads or glass
   noodles, soaked in cool water
   for 10 minutes (see Note)
1 fennel bulb, trimmed and diced
   (1 cup)
4 scallions (white and green parts),
   finely chopped
1 stalk lemongrass, tough outer
   layers and green parts removed,
   minced
1¾ pounds small Yukon Gold
   potatoes, not peeled
3 metal skewers
Vegetable oil spray
One 3-inch chunk fresh turmeric or
   1 small carrot
4 jumbo eggs

Makes 6 servings

Make the Dressing

1. Put the cumin seeds in a small skillet and dry-roast over medium-high heat, sliding the skillet back and forth over the burner to prevent burning, until the cumin exudes a pleasant aroma, about 1 minute. Remove from the heat. Let cool, then grind in a spice grinder. Set aside.

2. Heat the oil in a medium skillet over high heat for 1 minute. Add the onion and sauté until limp. Season with the sugar, cayenne, salt, cumin, and fish sauce, and stir until the sugar and salt are dissolved. Transfer to a bowl and let cool. Add the lime juice to the dressing and stir to mix. Set aside.

Make the Salad

3. Mound the charcoal in one side of the grill, leaving the other side empty. Heat the grill.

4. While waiting for the grill to get hot, drain the bean threads. Add to a pot of boiling water and cook for 5 to 6 seconds, then drain and rinse with cool water. Squeeze to extract the excess water.

5. Cut the bean threads into 2-inch lengths and put in a large bowl. Add the fennel, scallions, and lemongrass. Toss gently. Cover and set aside.

6. Thread 5 to 6 potatoes onto each metal skewer. Spray generously with vegetable oil and place on the grill over medium-high heat. Grill, turning occasionally to prevent burning, until the potatoes are slightly charred and tender when pierced with a knife, about 20 minutes. Meanwhile, put the turmeric on the grill. Grill, turning occasionally, until slightly charred, about 15 minutes. Lay the eggs on the empty side of the grill, without coals, and turn occasionally until the shells turn slightly dark and the eggs are cooked, about 20 minutes. Remove everything from the grill and let cool.

7. Cut the potatoes into 1-inch chunks and place in the bowl with the bean threads. Peel the turmeric, cut into thin slivers, and add to the bowl. Peel the eggs and slice into bite-sized wedges. Add to the bowl.

8. Pour the dressing over and mix well. Transfer to a serving platter.

Note: For more information on bean threads, or glass noodles, see page 104.

Grilled Shrimp Salad

AYUDHYA, THE ANCIENT CAPITAL of Thailand, is famous for big river prawns that are available all year round. Often served simply grilled, or with a spicy, sweet-and-sour sauce, the prawns also make a cool summer salad. Here I substitute large shrimp, which are easier to find.

Dressing

Makes ⅓ cup

1½ tablespoons granulated sugar

1 tablespoon palm sugar or maple sugar

½ teaspoon sea salt

2 tablespoons fish sauce (nam pla)

2 tablespoons tamarind juice (see page 137)

1 garlic clove, minced

4 red bird chiles or 3 serrano chiles, minced

2 tablespoons fresh lime juice

• • •

1 stalk lemongrass, tough outer layers and white parts removed; use only the tender green midsections

2 shallots, thinly sliced

5 thin slices young ginger, slivered (see Note)

4 kaffir lime leaves, slivered, or slivered zest of 1 lime

1 cup cilantro leaves, coarsely chopped

12 mint leaves, torn and bruised

1½ pounds large shrimp, peeled, deveined, and thoroughly dried

10 bamboo skewers, soaked in water for 30 minutes, then dried

Vegetable oil spray

6 to 7 red or green leaf lettuce leaves

Makes 6 servings

Make the Dressing

1. Combine the granulated sugar, palm sugar, salt, fish sauce, and tamarind juice in a small saucepan. Heat over medium heat until the sugars and salt are dissolved. Remove from the heat and let cool.

2. Add the garlic, chiles, and lime juice. Mix well and set aside.

Make the Salad

3. Mound the charcoal in one side of the grill, leaving the other side empty. Heat the grill.

4. While waiting for the grill to get hot, thinly slice the lemongrass on the diagonal. Separate into rings. Place in a bowl and add the shallots, ginger, kaffir lime leaves, cilantro, and mint. Mix well; cover with a damp towel and set aside.

5. Thread 3 to 4 shrimp onto each bamboo skewer. Spray generously with vegetable oil. Lay the shrimp on the grill over medium-high heat, arranging the skewers very close to one another. (The uncovered portion of the skewers should not be over the coals.) Grill, turning frequently, until the shrimp are pink and firm, 3 to 4 minutes. Transfer to a platter.

6. When the shrimp are cool enough to handle, remove from the skewers and add to the bowl with the herbs. Add the dressing and toss lightly. Transfer to a serving platter lined with the lettuce leaves.

Note: If fresh young ginger is unavailable, you can substitute mature ginger. Massage the sliced ginger with 1 tablespoon sea salt, and let rest for 15 minutes, then rinse and dry thoroughly.

Seared Ahi Tuna with Japanese Seaweed

HERE'S A CROSS-CULTURAL southern Italian–Japanese-style salad if there ever was one. It's easy to make, with surprises from both cuisines. The dressing can be made ahead and refrigerated for a couple of days. Have the greens mixed and ready, and grill the freshest fish you can find, just before serving. Chuka Salada, or Japanese seaweed in sesame oil, shichimi togarashi or Japanese chile pepper, and pickled ginger are available in Japanese and other Asian markets.

Make the Dressing

1. Combine all the ingredients in a bowl or jar and mix well. Set aside. Stored in a glass jar with a tight-fitting lid in the refrigerator, the dressing will keep for a couple of days.

Make the Tuna

2. Combine the ginger, garlic, miso, sugar, shichimi togarashi, mirin, and vegetable oil in a large bowl. Whisk to mix well. Add the tuna and coat well. Cover and refrigerate for 30 minutes.

3. Heat the grill and while waiting for it to get hot, combine the mushrooms, arugula, mizuna, red leaf lettuce, Chuka Salada, and pickled ginger in a bowl and toss gently. Cover with a dish towel and refrigerate.

4. Remove the tuna from the refrigerator and spray generously with vegetable oil. Place the tuna over medium-high heat. After 1 minute, carefully turn and brush with the remaining marinade. Cook until the outside is seared but the inside is still rare, about 5 minutes. Transfer to a plate.

5. Remove the bowl of vegetables from the refrigerator. When the tuna is just cool enough to handle, cut it into 1-inch cubes and add to the vegetables. Add the dressing and toss lightly. Transfer to a platter and serve.

Dressing

Makes ½ cup

½ teaspoon sea salt
2 garlic cloves, minced (1 tablespoon)
1 tablespoon sugar
1 tablespoon Dijon mustard
¼ cup red wine vinegar
3 tablespoons olive oil
1 tablespoon balsamic vinegar

• • •

1 tablespoon minced ginger
2 garlic cloves, minced (1 tablespoon)
3 tablespoons red miso
1 tablespoon sugar
1 tablespoon shichimi togarashi or Japanese chile pepper
¼ cup mirin (sweet rice wine)
2 tablespoons vegetable oil
1½ pounds ahi tuna, approximately 1 inch thick
1 cup firmly packed enoki mushrooms
1 cup firmly packed torn arugula leaves
1 cup firmly packed torn mizuna lettuce or dandelion greens
1 cup firmly packed torn red leaf lettuce leaves
1 cup Chuka Salada (Japanese seaweed in sesame oil)
1 tablespoon slivered pickled ginger
Vegetable oil spray

Makes 6 servings

Grilled Scallop and Asparagus Salad

THE BEAUTIFUL COLOR AND crunchy-sweet taste of asparagus have made them the latest craze in Thailand. Upscale restaurants in Bangkok add them to stir-fries as well as salads. In this recipe, asparagus complements the delicate texture of the grilled scallops.

Make the Dressing

1. Combine the granulated sugar, palm sugar, salt, and fish sauce in a small saucepan and heat over medium heat until the sugars and salt dissolve. Remove from the heat and let cool completely.

2. Add the ginger, lime juice, and orange juice. Mix well and set aside.

Make the Salad

3. Heat the grill.

4. While waiting for the grill to get hot, combine the kumquats, kaffir lime leaves, and chiles in a bowl. Toss lightly; set aside.

5. Put a fine-mesh grill rack on top of the regular rack. Generously spray the asparagus with vegetable oil and rub with the salt. Place the grill over medium heat and grill, turning frequently, until the outside is charred and the color has brightened, 3 to 4 minutes. Transfer to a serving platter.

6. When the asparagus is cool enough to handle, diagonally slice into bite-sized pieces. Add to the bowl with the kumquats.

7. Meanwhile, generously spray the scallops with vegetable oil and place on the fine-mesh rack. Grill, using a spatula to turn them occasionally, until slightly charred and firm to the touch, 5 to 6 minutes. Transfer to a platter.

8. When the scallops are cool enough to handle, slice each in half, and add to the bowl with the asparagus. Add the dressing, toss gently, and transfer to a serving platter.

Dressing

Makes ½ cup

1½ tablespoons granulated sugar
1 tablespoon palm sugar or brown sugar
½ teaspoon sea salt
2 tablespoons fish sauce (nam pla)
1 tablespoon minced ginger
3 tablespoons fresh lime juice
3 tablespoons fresh orange juice

• • •

6 kumquats, thinly sliced and seeded (½ cup), or ½ cup orange sections
5 kaffir lime leaves, slivered, or slivered zest of 1 lime
4 fresh bird chiles or 2 serrano chiles, slivered
1 pound asparagus, hard stem ends removed
Vegetable oil spray
1 teaspoon sea salt
1 pound large sea scallops

Makes 6 servings

Noodles, Rice, and Flatbread

ONE SUMMER in 1981, when I was teaching at San Diego State University, a Vietnamese colleague took me to lunch at a neighborhood restaurant. I wanted something cool and light, so he suggested a noodle dish with grilled pork. This was my introduction to Vietnamese cooking.

The bowl was layered with rice vermicelli, red leaf lettuce, and thin cucumber slices. The mound of stark white noodles glistened with thumb-sized pork chunks that had been marinated, grilled, and tossed with cilantro leaves, mint, and coarsely chopped peanuts. Somewhere in the flavor-packed bowl, I could smell lemongrass. My friend handed me a bowl of a clear sweet-sour-pungent sauce with slivers of carrots to spoon over the top. To this day, I can taste that first light, refreshing bite of slippery noodles and chewy grilled pork.

Since then I have eaten many variations of Vietnamese-style noodles. They remind me of the cool noodles my mother made during the hot season in Thailand. Instead of noodle soup, she served hand-rolled and cut wheat noodles, with a topping of slivers of grilled pork, chicken, cucumber, and radish. A pungent, aromatic sauce made with garlic, crushed red pepper, soy sauce, Chinese dark vinegar, and sesame paste accompanied the dish. Years later, a Japanese friend served me almost the same dish, but made with soba (buckwheat) noodles in place of homemade wheat noodles.

Although beloved throughout Asia, noodles take second place to the Asian passion for rice. Both regular long-grain rice and sticky rice mixed with other ingredients make delicious one-dish meals, as well as good use of leftover rice. Cooked long-grain rice is prepared in many creative ways, including frying and grilling, as well as tossing in salad.

In Asian countries, grilled rice is eaten as a snack or with other grilled dishes. It can be simply prepared by wrapping it in leaves such as banana leaves, then grilling, or it may be combined with cooked meat, chicken, seafood, or vegetables and seasoned with spicy curry paste or dried spices.

China and India—and the countries in between—must be the world's largest consumers of flatbread. There are hundreds of recipes for turning wheat, rice, or buckwheat flour and water into bread. There are many ready-made flatbreads available in Asian and

Middle Eastern markets, which make simple accompaniments for grilled meat, chicken, or vegetables and perfect wraps for grilled food. Because so many of these ready-made flatbreads are available, I have included only one recipe of my mother's, but not just for sentimental reasons—her flatbread is delicious and easy to make.

Laotian-Style Grilled Chicken with Rice Vermicelli Soup

RICE VERMICELLI, AVAILABLE IN Asian markets, is sometimes sold as Guilin vermicelli. Look for noodles with strands that resemble translucent spaghetti. These noodles take longer to cook than most other Asian noodles; when done, the strands are plump, white, and very slippery. It's easiest to eat these noodles with chopsticks. Traditional condiments include sugar, dried chile powder, fish sauce, hoisin sauce, and lime slices, served in small sauce bowls, so each person can season the dish to his or her own taste.

1. Preheat the oven to 375°F. Place the chiles, garlic, and shallots in separate squares of aluminum foil. Drizzle the oil over them, wrap in the foil, and place in the oven. When the chiles are crisp and blackened, about 15 minutes, remove from the oven and let cool, then mince. When the garlic and shallots are softened, 20 to 25 minutes, remove from the oven and let cool, then peel and mince.

2. Pound 1 teaspoon of the salt, garlic, and shallots in a mortar with a pestle into a paste. Add the roasted chiles and pound to combine. Add the galangal and pound to a fine paste.

3. Heat the chicken broth in a medium saucepan over high heat. When it is boiling, add the chile paste and lower the heat. Add the lemongrass, tomatoes, sugar, and fish sauce and bring to a boil. Lower the heat to a simmer, cover, and cook for 30 minutes until the broth is infused with herbs and spices. Keep warm.

4. Meanwhile, combine the remaining 1 teaspoon of salt, pepper, and oyster sauce in a zippered plastic bag. Seal it and mix well. Unseal the bag, add the chicken breasts, and toss to coat. Refrigerate for 30 minutes.

5. While the broth cooks, mound the charcoal in one side of the grill, leaving the other side empty. Heat the grill.

5 chiles de árbol
6 garlic cloves
2 shallots
2 tablespoons vegetable oil
2 teaspoons sea salt
1 tablespoon minced galangal
   or ginger
6 cups chicken broth
1 stalk lemongrass, green parts and
   tough outer layers removed,
   and cut in half
2 tomatoes, thinly sliced
1 tablespoon sugar
¼ cup fish sauce (nam pla)
1 tablespoon freshly ground black
   pepper
¼ cup oyster sauce
1½ pounds boneless, skinless
   chicken breasts or thighs, sliced
   into thin strips
One 14-ounce package rice
   vermicelli

10 to 12 bamboo skewers, soaked in water for 30 minutes, then dried

Vegetable oil spray

6 red or green leaf lettuce leaves, shredded

1 cucumber, peeled, seeded, and thinly sliced

12 watercress sprigs

¼ cup unsalted dry-roasted peanuts, coarsely chopped

1 cup mint leaves, torn and bruised

1 cup Thai basil leaves, torn and bruised

3 scallions (white and green parts), finely chopped

Makes 6 servings

6. While waiting for the grill to get hot, cook the rice vermicelli in a pot of boiling water for 15 minutes, or until soft. Drain in a strainer and rinse with cool water. Squeeze the noodles to extract all the excess water and transfer to a bowl. Cover and set aside.

7. Thread 5 to 6 pieces of chicken onto each skewer. Spray generously with vegetable oil and put the chicken on the grill over medium-high heat, arranging the skewers very close to each other. (The uncovered portion of the skewers should not be over the coals.) Grill, turning frequently, until the chicken is cooked, 6 to 7 minutes. Transfer to a platter and tent with aluminum foil to keep warm.

8. Cover the bottoms of each of six serving bowls with a couple pinches of lettuce, a few slices of cucumber, and one or two watercress sprigs. Top with the rice vermicelli. Spoon a couple of ladlefuls of the soup over the vermicelli in each bowl. Remove the chicken pieces from the skewers and add to the bowls. Garnish with the peanuts, mint, Thai basil, and scallions. Serve with the condiments listed above.

Soba Noodles with Grilled Vegetables and Sesame-Ginger Dressing

THIS COOL VEGETARIAN NOODLE dish is a perfect meal for a hot summer day. Since it is served at room temperature, you can prepare everything several hours ahead, then assemble it at the last minute. The dressing keeps overnight in the refrigerator.

Make the Dressing

1. Combine all the ingredients in a saucepan and heat over medium-low heat, stirring until the tahini is dissolved. Transfer to a bowl and set aside to cool. (To store, transfer the dressing into a glass jar with a tight-fitting lid; it will keep for a couple of days refrigerated. To serve, add 1 to 2 tablespoons water to the dressing and heat in a small saucepan until the sesame paste is dissolved. Let cool before serving.)

Make the Noodles

2. Heat the grill.

3. While waiting for the grill to get hot, combine the sugar, mirin, soy sauce, and sesame oil in a large bowl and whisk to mix. Add the mushrooms, leeks, asparagus, and snow peas. Toss lightly and set aside.

4. Put a fine-mesh grill rack over the regular rack. Put the mushrooms, leeks, and asparagus on the grill over medium-high heat and brush with the marinade. Grill the asparagus until they are slightly charred and the color has brightened, about 2 minutes. Grill the leeks until slightly charred and soft, about 3 minutes. Grill the mushrooms until slightly charred and soft, about 3 minutes. Transfer to a plate. Put the snow peas on the grill last and cook until the color brightens, about 1 minute.

5. When they are cool enough to handle, slice the asparagus, leeks, and mushrooms into thin diagonal slices. Set aside.

6. Cook the soba in a large pot of boiling water until soft, 3 to 4 minutes. Drain in a strainer and rinse well with cool water. Squeeze the noodles to extract all the excess water. Transfer to a bowl. Add the bean sprouts and grilled vegetables.

7. Just before serving, add the dressing to the noodles, and mix well.

Dressing

Makes ¾ cup

2 tablespoons minced ginger
¼ cup mirin (sweet rice wine)
1 tablespoon sugar
½ teaspoon sea salt
3 tablespoons tahini (sesame paste)
1 tablespoon cayenne pepper
3 tablespoons soy sauce
2 tablespoons rice vinegar
1 teaspoon sesame oil

. . .

1 tablespoon sugar
½ cup mirin (sweet rice wine)
3 tablespoons soy sauce
1 teaspoon sesame oil
6 shiitake mushrooms, stems removed
3 leeks
1 pound asparagus, tough stem ends removed
1 cup snow peas
2 bundles soba (buckwheat) noodles
2 cups bean sprouts

Makes 6 servings

Grilled Seafood and Bean Threads in Banana Pouches

BEAN THREADS, SOLD IN ASIAN MARKETS, are also known as glass noodles or mung bean threads. They are thin translucent strands bundled tightly and wrapped in cellophane. If possible, buy packages of bean threads that contain several individually tied 2-ounce bundles. Otherwise, unwrap the large bundle of bean threads inside a large paper bag. Loosen the strands and, using scissors, cut off the amount needed inside the bag. This prevents the noodles from scattering all over the place. Store unused bean threads in a zippered plastic bag.

Serve this delicate dish with Grilled Vegetables in Rice Paper (page 71). It's also good with cooked rice and Chayote Relish (page 155). To spice it up, serve with Chiles, Garlic, Fish Sauce, and Lime Juice (page 144).

1. Heat the grill.

2. While waiting for the grill to get hot, soak the noodles in cool water for 10 minutes, or until pliable. Drain and plunge into a pot of boiling water for 5 seconds. Drain in a strainer and rinse thoroughly in cool water. Squeeze the noodles, a handful at a time, to extract all the excess water before transferring to a large mixing bowl.

3. Using scissors, cut the noodles into manageable lengths. Stir in the shrimp and crabmeat. Add the sambal and fish sauce and mix to combine. Add the mint and cilantro and mix again.

4. Line an aluminum foil rectangle with a banana leaf. Spoon about a cup of the noodle mixture onto the center of the leaf, and fold it into a package. Wrap the aluminum foil over it to make a tight pouch. Repeat with the remaining ingredients.

5. Or if using the corn husks, line each piece of foil with 2 corn husks. Add the filling and cover with another corn husk. Wrap the aluminum foil around the corn husks to make into a tight pouch.

6. Put the pouches on the grill over medium heat. Grill, turning occasionally, for 15 minutes. Transfer the pouches to a plate, unwrap them, and serve with the lime wedges.

6 ounces bean threads

1 pound baby shrimp, peeled, deveined, and thoroughly dried

½ pound crabmeat, picked over for shells and cartilage

⅓ cup Tomato and Chile Sambal (page 146)

3 tablespoons fish sauce (nam pla)

1 cup mint leaves, torn and bruised

½ cup cilantro leaves, coarsely chopped

Six 9 × 12-inch pieces aluminum foil

Six 9 × 12-inch pieces banana leaves (see page 38), or 18 dried cornhusks, soaked in water for 20 minutes, then dried

2 limes, cut into wedges (optional)

Makes 6 servings

Steamed Rice

BEFORE IT IS GRILLED, the rice needs to be cooked. This is a basic recipe for steamed rice, used in several of the dishes in this book. Leftover rice makes better grilled and fried rice. To make a perfect pot of steamed long-grain jasmine rice, once the rice is washed and rinsed, spread the grains in the saucepan, place your hand on top of the rice, and pour water gently over your hand and the rice until it covers the middle knuckle of your middle finger. This is the exact amount of water to make rice that is fluffy, moist, and evenly cooked. Short-grain Japanese rice usually requires less water than long-grain rice.

2 cups Thai long-grain jasmine rice
    or short-grain Japanese rice
About 2 cups water (or 2 to
    3 tablespoons less for
    short-grain Japanese rice)

Makes 4 cups

1. To wash the rice, combine the rice and cold water to cover in a medium saucepan and swirl the grains around with your hands. Drain and repeat the process two more times.

2. Spread the grains inside the saucepan. Place one hand lightly on top of the rice and pour enough water over your hand and the rice to cover the middle knuckle of your middle finger. Set the pan over high heat and bring to a rapid boil. Lower the heat to medium-high and cook, uncovered, until the water has been absorbed and the steam has created holes in the surface of the rice, 7 to 10 minutes.

3. Turn the heat to low, cover the pan, and cook the rice until the top layer is moist and the rice grains are tender and have lost their sheen, about 10 minutes. If some grains remain shiny, add 1 to 2 tablespoons water, cover, and cook for another 3 to 5 minutes.

4. When the rice is cooked and uniform in color, turn off the heat. Fluff with a fork to separate the grains. Cover and let sit for 10 minutes before serving.

Cool Rice Noodles with Grilled Shrimp

THIS IS ONE OF MY FAVORITE Vietnamese noodle dishes. For an impressive presentation, splurge on jumbo-sized shrimp. You can also substitute chicken for the shrimp.

1. Combine the garlic, shallots, sugar, salt, pepper, wine, and fish sauce in a large zippered plastic bag. Seal and toss the bag back and forth to mix. Add the shrimp, seal, and toss once more. Refrigerate for 1 hour.

2. Mound the charcoal in one side of the grill, leaving the other side empty. Heat the grill.

3. While waiting for the grill to get hot, cook the rice noodles in a pot of boiling water for 3 to 4 minutes, or until soft. Drain through a strainer and rinse with cool water. Squeeze the noodles to extract all the excess water. Transfer to a bowl, cover, and set aside.

4. Remove the shrimp from the marinade and transfer the marinade to a bowl. Thread 4 to 5 shrimp onto each skewer from the tail through the body to the head. Generously spray the shrimp with vegetable oil. Put on the grill over medium heat, arranging the skewers very close to one another. (The uncovered portion of the skewer should not be over the coals.) Grill, turning and basting frequently with the reserved marinade, until the shrimp are slightly charred and cooked through, 3 to 4 minutes. Transfer to a plate and tent with aluminum foil to keep warm.

5. Place a couple of pinches of lettuce leaves and a few cucumber slices in each of six serving bowls. Top with the rice noodles. Add the carrots and daikon. Remove the shrimp from the skewers and add to the bowls. Top with mint leaves, scallions, and peanuts. Just before serving, drizzle 3 to 4 tablespoons or more of sweet-and-sour sauce. Add the chiles, if using, mix, and enjoy.

8 garlic cloves, minced
3 shallots, minced (½ cup)
1 tablespoon sugar
1 teaspoon sea salt
1 teaspoon freshly ground black pepper
¼ cup Chinese rice wine (Shaoxing) or dry vermouth
3 tablespoons fish sauce (nam pla)
1 pound large shrimp, peeled and deveined
8 ounces rice noodles (rice sticks)
6 to 7 bamboo skewers, soaked in water for 30 minutes, then dried
Vegetable oil spray
6 red or green leaf lettuce leaves, julienned
1 cucumber, peeled, halved lengthwise, seeded, thinly sliced
1 cup shredded carrots
1 cup shredded daikon
1 cup mint leaves
2 to 3 scallions (green and white parts), finely chopped
¼ cup unsalted dry-roasted peanuts, coarsely chopped
Triple recipe Vietnamese Sweet-and-Sour Sauce (page 149)
2 jalapeño chiles, thinly sliced (optional)

Makes 6 servings

Pineapple and Sweet Sausage Rice in Young Coconuts

SEVERAL YEARS AGO, my restaurant sold this as a take-out dish for Fourth of July picnics. Serve with Thai-Style Cucumber Relish (page 151) and pickled ginger.

Young coconuts are sold in Asian markets and some large supermarkets. They look like a white cylinder with pointed tops.

1 teaspoon white peppercorns
3 cups cooked Thai long-grain jasmine rice (see page 105)
1 cup vegetable oil
3 shallots, thinly sliced
1 teaspoon sea salt, plus a couple of pinches
3 garlic cloves, minced
2 to 3 cilantro stems with roots, minced
1 tablespoon minced ginger
1 medium onion, finely chopped
2 Chinese or Portuguese sweet sausages, grilled and thinly sliced
1 cup finely diced pineapple
2 tablespoons soy sauce
2 tablespoons fish sauce (nam pla)
3 young coconuts, tops sliced off and reserved, drained
Three 12 × 18-inch pieces aluminum foil

Makes 6 servings

1. Put the peppercorns in a small skillet and dry-roast over high heat, sliding the skillet back and forth over the burner to prevent burning, until the peppercorns exude a pleasant aroma, about 1 minute. Remove from the heat and let cool, then grind in a spice grinder. Transfer to a bowl and set aside.

2. Put the rice in a bowl and break up the clumps with your hands or a fork. Set aside.

3. Heat the oil in a large skillet over high heat for 1 minute. Add the shallots and stir for a minute or two, then add a couple of pinches of salt and stir until the shallots turn golden. Remove with a fine-mesh strainer to a plate lined with paper towels and let cool. Pour all but 2 tablespoons of the oil into a bowl and let cool before transferring to a jar with a tight-fitting lid; refrigerate and use for other stir-fry dishes. Set the skillet aside.

4. Heat the grill.

5. While waiting for the grill to get hot, pound the remaining 1 teaspoon salt and the garlic in a mortar with a pestle into a fine paste. Add the peppercorns and cilantro and pound into a paste. Transfer to a small bowl and set aside.

6. Heat the reserved 2 tablespoons of oil in the skillet over high heat. Add the spice paste and sauté for 10 to 15 seconds. Add the ginger, sauté for another 10 seconds, and add the onion. Stir-fry until the onion is limp and translucent. Add the rice, sausages, and pineapple and stir-fry for 10 seconds. Add the soy sauce and fish sauce and stir-fry until all the ingredients are well mixed. Remove from the heat.

7. Fill the coconuts with the fried rice and top with the crispy shallots. Cap the coconuts with the reserved tops and wrap in the aluminum foil. Place in the grill over medium heat and grill for 15 minutes. Cover the grill and grill for another 15 minutes. Be sure to open the air vents in the top of the grill cover.

8. Transfer the coconuts to a plate, unwrap the foil, and serve hot.

Curried Rice in Banana Leaves

TRY THIS RICE DISH as an accompaniment to grilled meat or chicken, or serve it with a salad for a light meal. Baked tofu cut into thin strips can be substituted for chicken.

1 cup vegetable oil

¾ cup thinly sliced shallots

1 teaspoon sea salt, plus a couple of pinches

4 garlic cloves, minced

½ pound boneless, skinless chicken breasts, sliced into thin strips

4 thin slices ginger, minced

1 tablespoon Madras curry powder

½ teaspoon freshly ground white pepper

¼ teaspoon cayenne pepper

2 tablespoons fish sauce (nam pla)

2 tablespoons soy sauce

4 cups cooked Thai long-grain jasmine rice (see page 105)

¼ cup coarsely chopped cilantro stems and leaves

½ cup mint leaves, torn

¼ cup finely chopped scallions (white and green parts)

Six 9 × 12-inch pieces banana leaves (see page 38), or 18 corn husks, soaked in water for 20 minutes, then dried

Six 12 × 24-inch pieces aluminum foil

Makes 6 servings

1. Heat the oil in a large skillet over high heat for 1 minute. Add ½ cup of the shallots, stirring constantly. Lower the heat to medium-high, add a couple of pinches of salt, and continue to stir until the shallots are golden. Remove with a fine-mesh strainer to a plate lined with paper towels and set aside.

2. Pour all but 2 tablespoons of the oil from the skillet into a bowl and let cool before transferring it to a glass jar with a tight-fitting lid. Refrigerate and reserve to use for other stir-fry dishes.

3. Heat the oil remaining in the skillet over high heat. Add the garlic and the remaining ¼ cup shallots and stir-fry until the garlic is golden and the shallots are translucent. Add the chicken and stir-fry until cooked through, 3 to 4 minutes. Add the ginger, the remaining 1 teaspoon salt, the curry powder, pepper, cayenne, fish sauce, and soy sauce, stirring to coat the chicken pieces well. Break up the clumps of rice before adding and stir-fry until well coated with the seasonings. Turn off the heat, add the cilantro, mint, and scallions; mix to combine. Remove from the heat and keep warm.

4. Heat the grill.

5. While waiting for the grill to get hot, line an aluminum foil rectangle with a banana leaf or 2 corn husks. Spoon a generous cup of the rice into the center. If using banana leaves, fold into a bundle, then wrap the aluminum foil around it to make a tight pouch. If using corn husks, place another corn husk on top of the rice and wrap the aluminum foil around the corn husks, forming a tight pouch. Repeat with the remaining ingredients.

6. Put the pouches on the grill over medium heat. Grill, turning occasionally, for 7 minutes. Transfer to a plate, and unwrap the pouches when ready to serve. Serve hot.

Grilled Tuna and Rice with Sesame and Bonito Shavings

ONE WINTRY WEEK, I visited my daughter, Angela, in New York City. While she was at work, I roamed around the city, and one day, I stumbled on a tiny Japanese restaurant, where I ordered a bowl of steaming miso soup. Instead of just a plain steamed Japanese rice, the soup was served with rice seasoned with katsuo mirin furikake, a seasoned dried bonito and sesame seed mix. It sparked the idea for this recipe. Serve with pickled ginger and Ponzu Sauce (page 148).

Katsuo mirin furikake is sold in Japanese and other Asian markets.

1. Combine the sugar and mirin in a small saucepan and cook over medium heat, stirring, until the sugar is dissolved. Transfer to a mixing bowl and add the rice. Mix well. Cover and let cool.

2. Add the katsuo mirin furikake to the cooled rice and mix well.

3. Heat the grill.

4. While waiting for the grill to get hot, combine the tuna with the soy sauce and sesame oil, tossing to coat. Line an aluminum foil rectangle with 3 corn husks. Spoon a cup of rice onto the center of the corn husks. Top with a couple pieces of tuna and a lemon slice. Lay a corn husk over the filling and wrap the aluminum foil around the corn husks, making a tight pouch. Repeat with the remaining ingredients.

5. Place the pouches on the grill over medium heat. Grill, turning frequently, until the tuna is cooked, about 7 minutes. Transfer to a plate, and unwrap the pouches when ready to serve. Serve hot.

2 tablespoons sugar

½ cup mirin (sweet rice wine)

6 cups warm cooked Japanese short-grain rice (see page 105)

1 cup katsuo mirin furikake (seasoned dried bonito and sesame seed mix)

½ pound ahi or yellowtail tuna, thinly sliced

2 tablespoons soy sauce

1 teaspoon sesame oil

6 thin lemon slices, seeded

Six 9 × 12-inch pieces aluminum foil

24 dried corn husks, soaked in water for 20 minutes, then dried

Makes 6 servings

Grilled Sticky Rice

THIS IS A GOOD WAY to use leftover sticky or regular long-grain rice, but fresh-cooked rice will also work fine. Serve with Grilled Shrimp Salad (page 93), any satay dish, or Grilled Fruit (page 123). This is also a convenient and unique way to serve rice at a picnic.

1. Soak the rice in cool water for at least 4 hours or overnight.

2. Drain the rice several times and wash with cool water. Line a steamer insert with 4 corn husks and spread the soaked sticky rice on top. Fill the pot about two-thirds full of water, just below steamer racks. Place the steamer insert in the pot, cover, and steam over medium-high heat for 15 to 20 minutes, or until the rice is tender. Transfer to a bowl and cover with a dish towel to keep warm.

3. Heat the grill.

4. While waiting for the grill to get hot, combine the salt and coconut cream in a saucepan and heat over high heat until warm. Pour over the rice and mix well. Cover with the dish towel and let sit for 10 minutes.

5. Line an aluminum foil square with a banana leaf. Put about ¾ cup of rice in the center. Fold the banana leaf into a package, then wrap the aluminum foil around it to form a tight pouch. Repeat with the remaining ingredients.

6. Or, if using corn husks, line each aluminum foil square with 2 corn husks. Put the rice in the center and top with another corn husk. Wrap the aluminum foil around the corn husks to form a tight pouch.

7. Place the pouches on the grill over medium-low heat. Grill, turning the pouches frequently, for 15 minutes. Transfer to a plate, and unwrap the pouches when ready to serve.

Variation: Substitute regular Thai long-grain jasmine rice for the long-grain sticky rice.

2 cups long-grain Thai jasmine
    sticky rice
¼ teaspoon sea salt
1 cup coconut cream
    (see page 135)
Six 12-inch squares aluminum foil
Six 9 × 12-inch pieces banana
    leaves (see page 38), or 22 corn
    husks, soaked in water for
    20 minutes, then dried

Make 6 servings

Chinese Flatbread with Scallions

EVERY SATURDAY, MY FAMILY ate Shantung-style pork and cabbage dumplings, and every Sunday, noodles or *pow-tze* (wheat buns with meat filling). No exceptions. When Mama prepared dumplings, she always made extra dough for flatbread with scallions. I love her flatbread even more than her dumplings.

3 cups all-purpose flour
⅔ cup water
1½ teaspoons sea salt
3 tablespoons sesame oil
½ cup finely chopped scallions
   (white and green parts)

Makes 3 flatbreads

1. Place 2 cups of the flour in a food processor. With the motor running, pour the water through the feed tube. Continue processing until a ball begins to form. Transfer the dough to a work surface.

2. Sprinkle 2 to 3 tablespoons of the flour over the dough. Knead for about 2 to 3 minutes, or until the dough is pliable but still soft. Sprinkle 1 tablespoon of the flour into a bowl, put the dough in it, and cover with a clean towel. Let rest for 20 minutes.

3. Heat the grill.

4. While waiting for the grill to get hot, divide the dough into 3 equal portions. Working with one portion at a time, roll out the dough using a rolling pin, sprinkling the dough at regular intervals with a couple of pinches of flour to prevent sticking, into a paper-thin 12-inch round. Sprinkle the round with ½ teaspoon of the salt and roll it gently into the dough. Spoon 1 tablespoon of the sesame oil into the center of the dough. Using a rubber spatula, spread the oil evenly over the entire surface. Cover the dough with one-third of the scallions.

5. Beginning with the edge closest to you, roll the dough into a long tight cylinder. Coil it into a round disk, pressing down with your hands to flatten. Roll it out once more into a 7- to 8-inch disk, approximately ¼ inch thick. Place the flatbread on wax paper sprinkled with flour and cover with a clean towel. Repeat the process with the remaining ingredients, placing each flatbread on wax paper sprinkled with flour.

6. Place a fine-mesh grill rack over the regular rack. Let the rack get hot before putting the flatbread on it. Grill over medium-low heat, flipping the breads frequently with a spatula to prevent burning, until the outside is crispy and the inside is firm and translucent, about 5 minutes. Keep warm. Cover with aluminum foil to keep warm.

7. When ready to serve, slice into bite-sized wedges.

Grilled Fruit and Vegetables

AMONG THE profusion of tropical fruit trees grown in Thailand, banana trees are the most common. City and country folk alike value them for their multiple uses. Food is wrapped for both cooking and storing in the broad iridescent green leaves. Young tender trunks lend a soft texture to spicy soups. The blossoms are picked for salads. But it's the fruit, the banana, with its soft sweet flesh, that is most prized.

Old people, as well as young babies, may live on a diet of grilled mashed bananas. When I was only five years old, my parents placed me in a boarding school. The meals were inedible, but twice a day, we were fed bananas. Because of this regime, I have great reverence for bananas and eat at least one a day.

In Thailand, Laos, Cambodia, and Myanmar (Burma), bananas are revered almost as much as rice and coconut. There are hundreds of banana varieties. Some are best eaten fresh, while others are best for cooking.

The simplest way to cook a banana is to grill the ripe fruit in its peel. When it is charcoal black, split the peel open to reveal a sweet, golden, aromatic custard. Markets throughout Thailand always have at least one vendor selling bananas prepared this way.

Slightly green bananas are peeled first, then grilled. When they are cooked and slightly charred, the vendor flattens the green bananas between a couple of pieces of peel and bathes them in a syrup made with sugar, salt, and coconut milk, then returns them to the grill. The pressed bananas take on the sweet perfume of the coconut, and their sugary taste is tempered with a touch of saltiness.

In Asia, grilling other fruits is also common, and it is preferred over slow cooking or baking with sugar. The process is quick and simple. Just add a couple of pinches of sugar, salt, and dried spices and/or coconut cream. Grilling alters the texture only slightly, enhancing the natural sweetness of the fruit. The sugar caramelizes, resulting in a smoky-sweet fruity flavor.

Fruits with firm flesh, such as pineapples, pears, peaches, and mangoes, are delicious when grilled. To grill fruit for dessert, be sure to use a brush to remove any grilled food residue from the grate. Nothing is worse than the flavor of fish or meat on your fruit!

Vegetables such as potatoes, sweet potatoes, squash, and corn are standard fare in Western grilling. But other vegetables, such as onion, tomato, asparagus, mushrooms, broccoli, and peppers, are great for variety. Instead of using butter or sour cream, salt, and pepper, grill them Asian-style, serving various sauces. Root vegetables and corn are delicious with a sweet-spicy-salty syrup, a mixture of granulated sugar, palm sugar, salt, and coconut cream. Cayenne pepper adds spiciness. The Chinese prefer cinnamon and star anise with rock candy for fruit, and soy sauce for vegetables. Indians, Malaysians, and Indonesians adore spice-laced syrups with nutmeg, mace, and cardamom for grilled fruit, and a variety of peppers for grilled vegetables.

Grilled Bananas

GRILLED BANANAS, a favorite Thai street snack, are sold in every market. Toss the sliced grilled bananas with some sliced fresh strawberries for variety, or use them as a topping for ice cream. Palm sugar is available in most Asian supermarkets or through mail-order sources.

1. Heat the grill.

2. While waiting for the grill to get hot, combine the granulated sugar, palm sugar, salt, and coconut cream in a saucepan and cook over medium heat, stirring until the sugars and salt are dissolved. Transfer to a bowl and set aside.

3. Place the unpeeled bananas on the grill over medium-low heat and cook and turn for 10 minutes, or until the peels are black. Transfer to a plate.

4. When they are cool enough to handle, peel the bananas and slice into 1-inch pieces. Add the bananas to the syrup, toss, and serve.

3 tablespoons granulated sugar
1 tablespoon palm sugar or
   brown sugar
1 teaspoon sea salt
½ cup coconut cream
   (see page 135)
6 firm but ripe bananas

Makes 6 servings

Grilled Plantains

THROUGHOUT SOUTHEAST ASIA, green bananas are grilled. Red bananas or plantains can be used for this recipe.

1. Heat the grill.

2. While waiting for the grill to get hot, combine the sugar, salt, and coconut milk in a saucepan and cook over medium heat until the sugar and salt are dissolved. Remove from the heat and add the grated coconut. Transfer to a bowl and set aside.

3. Slice each plantain into 3 equal pieces. Peel, but do not discard the peels. Place the plantains on the grill over medium heat. Grill for 5 minutes, turn frequently to prevent burning. Transfer to a plate.

4. Wrap the plantain in the reserved peel. Put another plate on top and press to flatten it. Repeat with the remaining plantains. Remove and discard the peels, dip each piece of flattened plantain in the syrup and return to the grill. Baste with the remaining syrup and grill for 2 to 3 minutes. Transfer to a plate and serve warm.

⅓ cup sugar
½ teaspoon sea salt
⅔ cup coconut cream
  (see page 135)
¼ cup grated coconut
  (see page 135)
3 plantains

Makes 6 servings

Grilled Fruit

SERVE THIS FRUIT MEDLEY on Ginger Ice Cream (page 124). Or for breakfast, try it with pancakes, waffles, or French toast. You can experiment with other soft fleshy fruits such as mango, nectarine, or plum, in addition to those suggested in the recipe. Palm sugar is available in most Asian supermarkets or through mail-order sources.

1 teaspoon cinnamon

1 teaspoon nutmeg

2 cups fresh pineapple chunks

2 cups strawberries, hulled

3 kiwis, halved

2 apricots, halved and pitted

2 medium peaches, halved and pitted

5⅓ tablespoons (⅓ cup) unsalted butter, melted

8 bamboo skewers, soaked in water for 30 minutes, then dried

½ cup palm sugar or brown sugar

1 teaspoon sea salt

½ cup combined coconut cream and milk (the consistency of whole milk) (see page 135)

Makes 6 servings

1. Heat the grill.

2. While waiting for the grill to get hot, combine ½ teaspoon each of the cinnamon and nutmeg in a large bowl. Add all the fruit and toss gently. Add the butter and toss again. Leaving the other fruits in the bowl, thread the pineapple chunks and strawberries onto separate skewers; set aside.

3. Combine the palm sugar, salt, the remaining ½ teaspoon each cinnamon and nutmeg, and the coconut cream mixture in a saucepan and cook over medium heat until the sugar is dissolved. Remove from the heat, cover, and set aside.

4. Lay a fine-mesh grill rack on top of the regular rack. Put the pineapple on the rack over medium heat. Grill, turning frequently to prevent burning, until slightly charred and soft, 6 to 7 minutes. Transfer to a plate and tent with aluminum foil to keep warm. Place the kiwis, apricots, and peaches over medium heat and grill, turning frequently with a spatula, until slightly charred and soft, about 6 minutes for the kiwis and apricots, 4 minutes for the peaches. Transfer to another plate and tent with aluminum foil to keep warm. Grill the strawberries for 2 to 3 minutes. Transfer to the same plate.

5. Remove the pineapple from the skewers and put in a bowl. Scoop the flesh of each kiwi from the peel. Slice in half and add to the bowl. Slice each apricot in half and add to the bowl. Peel the peaches, slice in half, and add to the bowl. Remove the strawberries from the bamboo skewers and add to the bowl. Pour the syrup over the fruit and toss lightly. Transfer to a bowl and serve.

Ginger Ice Cream

GINGER IS ONE OF the most popular herbs in Asia. Because it is believed to warm the lungs and aid circulation, there's no better way to end a meal than with a touch of ginger.

1. Combine the chopped ginger and water in a food processor and puree. Line a bowl with a piece of cheesecloth and pour the mixture into it. Gather up the cheesecloth and squeeze out as much juice as possible. Reserve the juice and discard the ginger.

2. Combine the half-and-half with the heavy cream in a medium saucepan and heat over medium heat until warm. Set aside.

3. Combine the egg yolks and sugar in the food processor and blend until creamy. With the motor running, pour in the cream in a steady stream. Blend for 2 minutes, then add the ginger juice. Blend for another minute. Transfer to a bowl and refrigerate until cold.

4. Pour into an electric ice cream maker and freeze following the manufacturer's instructions. During the last 10 minutes, as the ice cream is hardening, add the candied ginger. Freeze to firm.

1 cup chopped ginger with peel
½ cup water
2 cups half-and-half
1 cup heavy (whipping) cream
2 large egg yolks
1 cup sugar
1 cup minced candied ginger

Makes 1 generous quart

Coconut Ice Cream

THIS LUSH, SILKY ICE CREAM is scrumptious by itself, or as an accompaniment for grilled fruit.

3 cups coconut cream
  (see page 135)
1 cup half-and-half
4 large egg yolks
1 cup sugar

Makes 1 generous quart

1. Combine the coconut cream and half-and-half in a saucepan and heat over low heat, stirring constantly, until warm, about 7 minutes. Remove from the heat.

2. Whisk the egg yolks in a medium bowl until smooth. Add the sugar and whisk to combine. Continuing to whisk, pour the warm coconut cream in a steady stream into the mixture, and whisk until smooth and silken.

3. Transfer to a saucepan and heat over low heat, stirring constantly, until the mixture thickens. Do not boil or the mixture will curdle. Transfer to a bowl and refrigerate until chilled.

4. Transfer to an ice cream machine and freeze following the manufacturer's instructions. Freeze to firm.

Grilled Mangoes with Ginger Syrup

IN THAI HOMEOPATHIC TRADITION, mango is believed to possess an element that increases body temperature and heat. During the hot Southeast Asian summers, mangoes are most plentiful and at their prime. Yet old-timers caution that they should be eaten sparingly when the weather is hot, so as not to overheat one's system.

In America, mangoes start to arrive in late spring and continue throughout the summer. It is an ideal time to serve grilled mangoes with Ginger or Coconut Ice Cream (page 124 or 125). Rock sugar is available in most Asian markets.

1. Heat the grill.

2. While waiting for the grill to get hot, combine the sugar, water, and ginger in a saucepan and cook over high heat, stirring constantly, until the sugar is dissolved. Remove from the heat and let sit until cool. Strain the syrup into a bowl, discard the ginger, and set aside.

3. Peel the mangoes. Stand each one up and slice down on either side of the flat pit to remove the flesh in 2 large slices. Brush the mango slices with melted butter and put on the grill over medium heat. Grill, turning occasionally with a spatula and brushing with more butter, until slightly charred, 2 to 3 minutes. Transfer to a large bowl.

4. Add the ginger syrup to the mangoes and toss gently, then cover and let sit for 1 hour. Serve with the sprigs of mint, or with ice cream.

⅓ cup rock sugar
⅔ cup water
14 thin slices ginger, crushed
3 firm but ripe mangoes
3 tablespoons unsalted butter, melted
Sprigs of mint for garnish

Makes 6 servings

Grilled Asian Pears

MY PARENTS EMIGRATED FROM China to Thailand and lived there for forty-five years. Not a day passed that they did not speak of their homeland. They yearned for their favorite fruits, especially the Asian pear. After they moved to America, the first time they found the pears in an Asian market, they cried with joy. Every time I see Asian pears, I think of my parents. The crisp, crunchy, sweet, and juicy fruit, the size of a big apple, with a rough skin that looks like a brown paper bag, is usually eaten fresh. It retains its crispy texture with a sweet mellow taste when grilled. Substitute Comice or Taylor pears if necessary.

1. Heat the grill.
2. While waiting for the grill to get hot, combine the rock sugar, pineapple juice, ginger, star anise, and cinnamon stick in a saucepan and heat over high heat until the sugar dissolves and the liquid begins to boil, stir occasionally. Reduce the heat to medium-low and boil gently for 2 minutes. Remove from the heat and let cool.
3. Peel the pears, slice each one in half, and remove the cores. Place in a bowl and add the lemon juice. Toss gently, then add the butter.
4. Put a fine-mesh/grill rack on top of the regular rack. Place the pears on it over medium heat and grill, turning frequently to prevent burning, until slightly charred, 6 to 7 minutes. Transfer to a bowl, add the syrup, and mix well. Cover and let sit for 20 minutes before serving. For best results, refrigerate overnight. Bring to room temperature before serving.

⅓ cup rock sugar
½ cup pineapple juice
12 thin slices ginger
3 star anise
1 cinnamon stick
3 Asian pears
Juice of 1 lemon
3 tablespoons unsalted butter, melted

Makes 6 servings

Grilled Sweet Potatoes

GROWING UP IN CHINA, my father lived almost solely on sweet potatoes. Years of starvation and eating only this lowly vegetable evoked such painful memories later that sweet potatoes were not allowed in our home. My mother, however, loved sweet potatoes and occasionally would buy them grilled from street vendors.

3 sweet potatoes
1 cup coconut cream
   (see page 135)
1 teaspoon sea salt
1 teaspoon nutmeg
1 cup minced candied ginger

Makes 6 servings

1. Heat the grill.

2. Place the sweet potatoes on the grill over medium-high heat. Cover and grill for 50 minutes, or until the potatoes are slightly charred and the inside is soft and tender when pierced with a fork. Be sure to open the air vents in the top of the grill. Transfer to a plate, cover, and keep warm.

3. Combine the grated coconut cream, salt, and nutmeg in a small saucepan and cook over medium heat, stirring, until the cream comes to a boil. Remove from the heat.

4. Slice the sweet potatoes in half and scoop the flesh into a bowl. Reserve the shells. Mash and puree the sweet potatoes. Add the hot syrup and mix to combine, then beat until fluffy. Add all but 1 tablespoon of the candied ginger and mix to combine. Transfer the mashed sweet potatoes into the empty shells. Garnish with the reserved candied ginger and serve.

Grilled Pineapple with White Pepper and Palm Sugar

SERVE GRILLED PINEAPPLE warm or at room temperature. It's good by itself or with Coconut Ice Cream (page 125). Use ripe, sweet pineapple. Palm sugar is available in most Asian supermarkets or through mail-order sources.

1. Heat the grill.

2. While waiting for the grill to get hot, combine the palm sugar and coconut cream in a saucepan and cook over medium heat until the sugar is dissolved. Transfer to a bowl and set aside.

3. Sprinkle the white pepper over the pineapples and generously spray with vegetable oil. Place on the grill over medium heat and grill, turning frequently to prevent burning, until slightly charred and softened, about 7 minutes. Add to the bowl with the sauce and mix well. Cover and let sit for at least 15 minutes or longer, or refrigerate for up to a day, before serving.

½ cup palm sugar or brown sugar
½ cup coconut cream
  (see page 135)
1 teaspoon freshly ground white
  pepper
1 small pineapple, peeled, cored,
  and cut into ½-inch slices
Vegetable oil spray

Makes 6 servings

Grilled Corn

AS A FOREIGN STUDENT attending school in Kentucky, I was introduced to corn for the first time. During the summer, as far as the eye could see, the green fields surrounding my school were lined with endless rows of ripening corn. For a couple of dollars, you could pick enough corn to feed an army. Instead of the American tradition of butter, salt, and pepper, here's a Thai way of dressing up fresh corn.

1. Heat the grill.

2. While waiting for the grill to get hot, heat the coconut cream in a saucepan over medium heat until warm. Remove and let cool completely

3. Add the grated coconut, cayenne, salt, and lemon zest to the coconut cream. Transfer to a bowl.

4. Grill and turn the corn over medium heat until the color brightens and it is slightly charred, about 5 minutes. Remove from the grill and coat with the coconut mixture. Place the corn back on the grill and cook, turning frequently, for 1 minute. Repeat the coating and grilling process 3 to 4 times, grilling for a total of 12 minutes. Transfer to a serving platter and serve hot.

6 ears corn, husked
1 cup coconut cream
   (see page 135)
½ cup grated coconut
   (see page 135)
1 teaspoon cayenne pepper
1 teaspoon sea salt
Grated zest of 1 lemon

Makes 6 servings

Seasonings, Sauces, and Condiments

IN ASIAN COOKING, seasoning and dipping sauces are the magic potions that transform ordinary food into irresistible delicacies. They are the alchemy, the chef's personal signature, that adds the yin and yang, or balance, to dishes.

My mother, an extraordinary self-taught cook, told stories about the fanatical measures ancient Chinese cooks took to guard their secret recipes. There are tales of legendary Thai cooks who took their cooking secrets to the grave rather than share them with others. Often even close family members can't get a family recipe. But, sooner or later, most secrets get told, and this is certainly true of the seasonings and dipping sauces used in Asian cooking. As Asian food has become more popular, bottles and cans of ready-made so-called secret seasonings and sauces are increasingly available to those who want to take a shortcut when preparing Asian dishes. However, if you want authentic flavors, you must mix and blend your own seasonings, herbs, and spices. Asian food is seldom seasoned with just salt and pepper, and this is especially true when grilling. Store-bought sauces and seasonings have nothing of the freshness that makes Asian food so tasty and extraordinary.

These dipping sauces and condiments are accompaniments to be served with the recipes in the book. Any of them will add spice and variety to your own favorite barbecue creations as well.

The ingredients discussed in the following sections can be bought ready-made in Asian markets and specialty gourmet shops, but homemade is always better. These are easy to make, and most can be stored in the refrigerator or pantry, ready to be used for a variety of dishes.

Coconut Milk and Cream

THESE STAPLES ARE USED in most Southeast Asian cooking. In grilling, they are used as cooking oil as well as a tenderizer. Although canned coconut milk and cream can be purchased in supermarkets, the freshly made can't be matched for flavor. The pasteurization process used in canning strips away the enzymes needed for the rich coconut oil flavor. The real thing also has an aroma that can't be purchased. Coconut milk is easy to prepare and can be stored in the freezer for future use.

The coconut pieces can also simply be grated, following the instructions below, then stored and used to add a crunchy-nutty texture to almost any recipe. The husks and dark peels of fresh coconuts also make good kindling for grill-smoking.

1 coconut
4 cups hot water

Makes approximately 1 cup cream plus 3 cups milk

1. Preheat the oven to 350°F. Pierce a hole in each of the three eyes in the top of the coconut, using a Phillips screwdriver and a hammer. Drain the juice and discard. Place the coconut in the oven and bake for 15 minutes. Remove and cool.

2. With a hammer, crack and shatter the coconut into manageable pieces.

3. Wrap one hand in a thick dish towel. Holding a piece of coconut firmly, pry the flesh off the husk with a paring knife. Repeat with the remaining coconut. Peel the dark hard outer skin from the white flesh with a vegetable peeler. Cut the coconut into 1-inch cubes. (Do not dis-

card the hard peels. Instead, put them on a tray to dry in the sun for several days, and set aside for grill-smoking food.)

4. With the motor running, drop the coconut pieces into a food processor and grind for 3 to 4 minutes, until the coconut resembles oatmeal flakes. (If preparing grated coconut, it is ready to be used.)

5. With the machine running, add 1 cup of the hot water and process for 2 to 3 minutes. Transfer to a mixing bowl and add the remaining 3 cups hot water. Let the mixture stand until cool enough to handle. Massage the grated coconut for 3 to 4 minutes, or until the water turns white like whole milk.

6. Place a fine-mesh strainer over a bowl. Extract the milk from the coconut by squeezing the grated coconut a handful at a time over the strainer. Reserve the grated coconut for other uses such as making coconut macaroons. Cover the coconut milk and cream and refrigerate for 20 minutes.

7. Skim off the heavy cream that has risen to the top of the coconut to use according to the instructions in the recipes; store it in a zippered plastic bag and refrigerate or freeze. The remaining clear liquid is the coconut milk. Use immediately, or store in a separate zippered plastic bag in the refrigerator or freezer. It will keep for a month.

Tamarind Juice

FRUITY, TANGY TAMARIND JUICE is a perfect seasoning for Southeast Asian cooking. It also acts as a meat tenderizer. Bottled tamarind juice is sometimes available in Asian markets, but it has artificial additives and an off taste. Blocks of dried tamarind pulp are sold in Asian markets.

One 4 × 3-inch chunk tamarind
    pulp
1¼ cups boiling water

Makes 1 cup

1. Combine the tamarind pulp and boiling water in a bowl. Let sit until the water is cool to the touch. Massage the tamarind to loosen and separate the pods, then let sit for another 15 minutes and massage it once more.

2. Wait for another 15 minutes, or until the thickened liquid looks like applesauce. Skim off the amount called for in the recipe. Transfer the rest to a glass jar with a tight-fitting lid and refrigerate. It will keep for a couple of weeks. Each time you use it, add some cold water to the juice. When it becomes too watery and will no longer thicken when you add water, discard it, and start a new batch.

Szechwan Red Chile Oil

TRUE SZECHWAN PEPPERS are spicy and numbing. Used as medicine as well as for cooking, they are sold in Chinese medicinal shops instead of markets. Unfortunately, there is no substitute for this special pepper. You can buy ready-made reddish-colored chile oil in Asian markets, but there is no match for the homemade version of this aromatic, spicy flavoring.

1. Dry-roast the Szechwan peppercorns in a small skillet over medium-high heat, sliding the skillet back and forth over the burner to prevent burning, until they begin to exude a pleasant aroma, 1 to 2 minutes. Transfer to a bowl. Repeat the process with the red pepper, toasting it for 1 minute. Add to the Szechwan peppercorns and set aside.

2. Heat the oil in a large skillet over medium-high heat until it begins to smoke. Reduce the heat to low, add the scallions and ginger, and stir until they are limp, 1 to 2 minutes. Add the Szechwan peppercorns and red pepper and stir and cook until the oil turns red. Transfer to a bowl and let cool.

3. Place a fine sieve over another bowl. Pour the oil through the sieve into the bowl and discard the solids. Transfer the oil to a glass jar with a tight-fitting lid. Store at room temperature for 2 to 3 weeks.

½ cup Szechwan peppercorns
½ cup crushed red pepper
2 cups vegetable oil
2 scallions (white and green parts), sliced
8 thin slivers ginger

Makes about 1⅓ cups

Garam Masala

GARAM MASALA IS AN Indian spice blend. There are countless variations, depending on the region where the recipe originated. Garam masala can be bought in Indian and Middle Eastern markets, as well as gourmet specialty shops and through mail-order sources.

Not only is homemade garam masala simple to make but the perfume produced by the freshly dry-roasted herbs and spices is far better than any that can be bought in a store.

¼ cup coriander seeds
2 tablespoons cumin seeds
1 tablespoon black peppercorns
2 teaspoons cardamom pods
Two 3-inch cinnamon sticks,
  broken into small pieces
1 teaspoon whole cloves
1 nutmeg

Makes approximately ½ cup

1. Dry-roast the coriander seeds in a small skillet over medium heat, sliding the skillet back and forth over the burner to prevent burning, until the seeds exude a pleasant aroma, 1 to 2 minutes. Transfer to a bowl and set aside. Repeat the process, one at a time, with the cumin seeds, peppercorns, cardamom, cinnamon, and cloves. Let cool completely.

2. Put all the ingredients except the nutmeg in a spice grinder and grind to a fine powder. Transfer to a bowl. Grate the nutmeg over the mixture. Stir to mix well. Transfer to a glass jar with a tight-fitting lid. The garam masala will keep at room temperature for at least a month.

Five-Spice Powder

THIS FAMOUS FIVE-SPICE seasoning mix is used to flavor meat and poultry dishes in Chinese cooking. With a spice (or coffee) grinder, it is easy to make.

1. Dry-roast the peppercorns in a small skillet over medium heat, sliding the skillet back and forth over the burner to prevent burning, until they exude a pleasant aroma, 1 to 2 minutes. Transfer to a bowl and set aside to cool. Repeat the process, one at a time, with the remaining ingredients.

2. Put all the ingredients into a spice grinder and grind to a fine powder. Let the powder stand in the machine for a minute before transferring it to a glass jar with a tight-fitting lid. It will keep in the pantry for up to a month.

2 tablespoons black peppercorns
3 star anise
2 teaspoons fennel seeds
Two 3-inch cinnamon sticks,
    broken into small pieces
6 whole cloves

Makes approximately ¼ cup

Dipping sauces, the Asian equivalent of mustard and ketchup, heighten and accentuate the flavors of grilled meat, chicken, and seafood. Each country has its own preferences, carefully selected to match specific dishes.

Indonesian Peanut Sauce

IF YOU LOVE PEANUT sauce, use this robust and flavorful version as a dipping sauce for satay or as a dressing for a warm salad.

1 teaspoon sea salt

2 garlic cloves, minced
(1 tablespoon)

12 chiles de árbol or chiles Japonés, softened in hot water, dried, seeded, and minced

1 tablespoon minced galangal or ginger

1 stalk lemongrass, tough outer layers and green parts removed, minced (¼ cup)

2 shallots, minced (¼ cup)

1 teaspoon red miso

3 tablespoons vegetable oil

¼ cup plus 1 tablespoon sugar

¼ cup creamy peanut butter

½ cup coconut cream
(see page 135)

¼ cup tamarind juice
(see page 137)

Makes 1 cup

1. Pound the salt and garlic in a mortar with a pestle into a fine paste. Add the chiles and pound to a puree. One at a time, add the galangal, lemongrass, shallots, and red miso, in sequence, adding each one only after the previous ingredient has been completely pureed and incorporated into the paste. Transfer to a bowl or to a glass jar with a tight-fitting lid. Refrigerated, the seasoning paste will keep for a month.

2. Or, if using a blender, add all the above ingredients plus the vegetable oil and puree.

3. Sauté the chile paste in the oil (or the chile paste-oil mixture) in a saucepan over medium-high heat until it exudes a pleasant aroma, about 2 to 3 minutes. Lower the heat and add the sugar, peanut butter, coconut cream and tamarind juice. Stir to mix, and heat until the mixture boils and thickens, about 2 minutes.

4. Transfer to a bowl and let cool before serving. Stored in a glass jar with a tight-fitting lid in the refrigerator, the sauce will keep for a couple of weeks. If it congeals and thickens, dilute with 2 to 3 tablespoons water and cook over low heat in a saucepan, stirring until smooth.

Thai Sweet Pepper Sauce

ONCE YOU TASTE THIS SAUCE, I guarantee you will love it as much as my restaurant customers do. It is marvelous with grilled chicken or shrimp, and fabulous as a basting sauce for baked ham or lamb.

Heat the oil in a medium saucepan over high heat for 1 to 2 minutes. Add the garlic and cook, stirring to prevent burning, until it turns yellow. Add the remaining ingredients and stir and cook, stirring, until the sauce boils and the sugar is completely dissolved. Boil for 8 minutes until the mixture easily coats a spoon. Then transfer to a serving bowl and let cool; the sauce will thicken like maple syrup. Or transfer to a glass jar with a tight-fitting lid and store in the refrigerator for up to a month.

1 tablespoon vegetable oil
1 garlic clove, minced
½ cup sugar
½ teaspoon sea salt
¾ cup cider or white vinegar
1 teaspoon crushed red pepper
1 teaspoon cayenne pepper

Makes ¾ cup

Thai Vegetarian Peanut Sauce

ALTHOUGH THIS PEANUT SAUCE IS FOR VEGETARIANS, carnivores will love it too. Unlike the Indonesian version, it is light, with a fruity taste and a nice floral scent. Use it with tofu, chicken, or shrimp satay. Palm sugar is available in most Asian supermarkets or through mail-order sources.

½ teaspoon sea salt

4 garlic cloves, minced
(2 tablespoons)

15 chiles de árbol or chile japonés,
softened in hot water, dried,
seeded or not, depending on
your preference for spiciness,
and minced (⅓ cup)

1 stalk lemongrass, tough outer
layers and green parts removed,
minced (¼ cup)

1 tablespoon minced galangal or
ginger

2 shallots, minced (¼ cup)

1 cup combined coconut cream
and milk (the consistency of
whole milk) (see page 135)

1 tablespoon soy sauce

3 tablespoons palm sugar or
brown sugar

2 tablespoons creamy peanut
butter

3 tablespoons tamarind juice
(see page 137)

Makes 1 cup

1. Pound the salt and garlic in a mortar with a pestle into a fine paste. One at a time, add the chiles, lemongrass, galangal, and shallots, in sequence, adding each one only after the previous ingredient has been pureed and incorporated into the paste.

2. Or, if using a blender, combine all the above ingredients, add the coconut cream mixture, and puree.

3. Combine the chile paste and coconut cream (or the chile paste–coconut cream mixture) in a saucepan over medium-low heat and cook, stirring constantly to prevent the coconut cream from curdling, until the mixture begins to bubble, 2 to 3 minutes. Add the soy sauce, palm sugar, and peanut butter and cook, stirring to dissolve the sugar and peanut butter. When the mixture begins to boil, add the tamarind juice. Stir to mix. Cook until the liquid begins to boil again. Transfer to a bowl and let cool before serving. Or store in a glass jar with a tight-fitting lid in the refrigerator for up to a week.

Chiles, Garlic, Fish Sauce, and Lime Juice

THIS CLASSIC DIPPING SAUCE once appeared on every Thai table. Today, the garlic is usually omitted. Either way, use it to season plain rice, noodles, soup, curry, and of course, grilled meat, poultry, seafood, and vegetables.

In a small mixing bowl, combine all the ingredients. To store, transfer to a glass jar with a tight-fitting lid and refrigerate; the sauce will keep for a week or two. Add more lime juice before serving if needed.

7 fresh bird chiles or 5 serrano chiles, thinly sliced
2 garlic cloves, thinly sliced
⅓ cup fish sauce (nam pla)
2 tablespoons fresh lime juice, or more to taste

Makes ½ cup

Wasabi Mayonnaise

MAYONNAISE SURPRISINGLY IS VERY POPULAR throughout Asia. Wasabi mayonnaise, with a hint of Japanese influence, complements grilled seafood, as well as adds zing to a salad dressing. The mint or basil-flavored variation is refreshing and a perfect match for both strong-flavored meats such as lamb or beef and delicate, subtle scallops.

½ teaspoon sea salt
2 garlic cloves, minced
1 large egg
1 egg yolk
2 tablespoons wasabi powder
1 tablespoon fresh lemon juice
¾ cup vegetable oil
2 tablespoons olive oil

Makes 1 cup

1. Pound the salt and garlic in a mortar with a pestle into a paste. Transfer to a food processor and add the egg, egg yolk, wasabi powder, and lemon juice. Process for 1 to 2 minutes, or until thoroughly mixed.

2. Combine the vegetable and olive oils. With the food processor running, slowly add the oil in a thin steady stream, processing until the mayonnaise thickens. Scrape down the sides of the bowl and process until thoroughly blended. Transfer to a glass jar with a lid and refrigerate. The mayonnaise is best within a few hours after it's made, but it will keep in the refrigerator for a couple of days.

Mint or Basil Mayonnaise Omit the wasabi powder and add 1 cup mint or Thai or Italian basil leaves, finely chopped.

Tomato and Chile Sambal

USE THIS TASTY SAUCE on grilled meat, poultry, and vegetables. Try it instead of ketchup on hamburgers, or with rice or pasta.

1. Heat the oil in a small saucepan over medium-high heat until it begins to smoke, 1 to 2 minutes. Add the shallots and garlic and stir-fry until limp and lightly browned. Add the chiles and stir-fry for another minute or two until fragrant. Add the tomato paste, water, molasses, salt, and pepper. Stir to mix, and bring to a boil.

2. Transfer to a bowl and let cool; serve lukewarm or cold. Stored in a glass jar with a tight-fitting lid in the refrigerator, the sauce will keep for a week.

3 tablespoons vegetable oil
6 shallots, minced (1 cup)
4 garlic cloves, minced
   (2 tablespoons)
30 fresh red bird chiles or 18 red
   serrano chiles, minced
   (use fewer chiles for a milder
   sauce)
⅓ cup tomato paste
¼ cup water
1 tablespoon molasses
1 teaspoon sea salt
½ teaspoon freshly ground black
   pepper

Makes ¾ cup

Chile and Soy Sambal

THIS SAUCE IS EXCELLENT with grilled meat and poultry. It keeps well in the refrigerator for a couple of days, but the lime flavor may lose strength, so taste before serving and add more lime juice if needed.

¼ cup soy sauce

2 to 3 tablespoons water

1 tablespoon molasses

2 shallots, minced

2 garlic cloves, minced

18 fresh bird chiles or 9 serrano chiles, thinly sliced crosswise (use fewer chiles for a milder sauce)

2 tablespoons fresh lime juice, or more to taste

Makes ⅓ cup

1. Combine the soy sauce, water, molasses, shallots, and garlic in a saucepan and stir over medium heat until the mixture boils. Reduce the heat and simmer, stirring for 5 minutes. Remove from the heat and let cool.

2. Add the chiles and lime juice to the sambal and stir to mix. Serve, or transfer to a glass jar with a tight-fitting lid and store in the refrigerator for up to 3 days.

Ponzu Sauce

TRADITIONAL JAPANESE PONZU SAUCE, or dressing, is made from the juice of a citrus fruit called yuzu. It complements traditional Japanese grilled fish or shrimp dishes. It is not easy to find yuzu, but you can substitute lime juice.

1. Combine the mirin, vinegar, soy sauce, and bonito flakes in a saucepan and bring to a boil over medium heat. Remove from the heat and let cool.

2. Pour the sauce through a strainer into a bowl; discard the bonito flakes. Add the lime juice. Serve, or store in a glass jar with a tight-fitting lid in the refrigerator for up to 3 days. Add more lime juice if needed before serving.

3 tablespoons mirin (sweet rice wine)
2 tablespoons rice vinegar
1 tablespoon soy sauce
2 tablespoons bonito flakes
¼ cup fresh yuzu or lime juice, or more to taste

Makes ½ cup

Vietnamese Sweet-and-Sour Sauce

THIS SAUCE ACCOMPANIES MANY Vietnamese dishes. It is used not only as a dipping sauce but also as a dressing for salads and cool noodle dishes.

1 garlic clove, minced

3 tablespoons sugar

5 fresh bird chiles or 2 red serrano chiles, minced

3 tablespoons fish sauce (nam pla)

2 tablespoons fresh lime juice

Makes ¼ cup

Pound the garlic and sugar in a mortar with a pestle into a paste. Add the chiles and pound to crush them. Transfer to a small bowl and add the fish sauce and lime juice. Mix well and taste. If the sauce is too pungent, add 1 to 2 tablespoons water. Serve, or store in a glass jar with a tight-fitting lid in the refrigerator for up to 3 days. Add more lime juice if needed.

Vietnamese Sweet-and-Sour Sauce with Tamarind Juice This variation goes well with Grilled Shrimp on Sugarcane Stalks (page 34) or Vietnamese Style Grilled Beef in Lettuce (page 60), or serve it as a sauce for egg rolls.

Add 1 tablespoon tamarind juice (see page 137) and 2 tablespoons unsalted dry-roasted peanuts, coarsely chopped, to the sauce and mix well. (Makes ½ cup.)

Condiments

Condiments made from vegetables and fresh herbs go hand in hand with Asian grilled dishes. Grilled dishes are always served with several condiments. Eaten together, the refreshing and cool-tasting condiments enhance and balance the flavors of hot and sizzling grilled dishes.

Raita – Cucumber in Spiced Yogurt

THE REFRESHING COMBINATION of cool cucumbers and creamy yogurt makes this a perfect side dish for Indian or Middle Eastern grilled food.

1. Using the side of a cheese grater with the large holes, grate the cucumber until you reach the seeds, turning the cucumber as necessary; discard the seedy center. Put the cucumber in a colander and add 1 teaspoon of the salt. Mix lightly and let sit for 30 minutes.

2. Rinse the cucumber with cool water. Squeeze to remove all the excess liquid. Combine the cucumber, grated coconut, chiles, the remaining 1/2 teaspoon of salt, and the yogurt in a bowl. Mix well and set aside.

3. Heat the ghee in a small covered saucepan over medium heat for 1 minute. Add the mustard seeds and stir-fry until they pop. Remove from the heat and pour over the yogurt and cucumber mixture. Mix and serve, or refrigerate. The raita will keep overnight.

1 English cucumber
1 1/2 teaspoons sea salt
1/4 cup grated coconut
  (see page 135)
2 to 3 serrano chiles, seeded or
  not, depending on your
  preference for spiciness,
  minced
3/4 cup yogurt
1 tablespoon ghee (clarified butter)
  or vegetable oil
1 teaspoon black mustard seeds

Makes 1 1/2 cups

Thai-Style Cucumber Relish

THIS CRISPY SWEET-AND-SOUR RELISH with a touch of spiciness is served with satay and spicy curries.

2 tablespoons fresh lime juice

1 tablespoon fish sauce (nam pla)

⅓ cup sugar

½ teaspoon sea salt

4 fresh bird chiles or 1 serrano chile, slivered

3 pickling (kirby) cucumbers, peeled, halved lengthwise, seeded, and thinly sliced on the diagonal

1 shallot, thinly sliced

2 tablespoons coarsely chopped cilantro

1 tablespoon coarsely chopped mint

1 tablespoon unsalted dry-roasted peanuts, coarsely chopped

Makes 1½ cups

1. Combine the lime juice, fish sauce, sugar, salt, and chiles in a bowl and mix well. Add the cucumber and shallot, and toss lightly. Let sit for 10 minutes.

2. Transfer the relish to a serving bowl, garnish with the cilantro, mint, and peanuts, and serve.

Indonesian-Style Cucumber Relish

LIGHT AND DELICATE, this relish is a great accompaniment to any grilled dish, including satay. It's even good with just plain cooked rice.

1. Combine the cucumber with ½ teaspoon of the salt in a colander. Toss lightly, and let stand in the sink for 15 minutes.

2. Rinse the cucumbers with cool water and dry thoroughly with a dish towel. Transfer to a bowl, add the onion, chiles, sugar, the remaining 1 teaspoon salt, and the vinegar. Mix to combine. Let stand for 15 minutes then serve.

3 pickling (kirby) cucumbers, peeled, halved lengthwise, seeded, and thinly sliced on the diagonal

1½ teaspoons sea salt

⅓ cup finely chopped onion

4 fresh bird chiles or 2 serrano chiles, minced (1½ teaspoons)

2 tablespoons sugar

¼ cup white vinegar

Makes 1 cup

Burmese Cucumber Relish

THE FIRST TIME I made this relish, I had some reservations as to the way I'd been told how to prepare the cucumber. And yet it remained crisp despite the long marinating period. Packed with subtle sweet and spicy flavors, colored a vibrant golden hue with the turmeric, it's a wonderful accompaniment to any spicy grilled dish.

¼ cup sesame seeds
1 English cucumber, halved lengthwise, seeded, and thinly sliced on the diagonal
½ cup julienned ginger
½ cup sugar
1 tablespoon plus ½ teaspoon sea salt
¼ cup cider or white vinegar
3 tablespoons vegetable oil
1 small yellow onion, halved and thinly sliced into strands (1½ cups)
½ teaspoon turmeric powder

Makes 2 cups

1. Put the sesame seeds in a small skillet and dry-roast over medium-high heat, sliding the skillet back and forth over the burner to prevent burning, until the sesame seeds turn golden, 1 to 2 minutes. Remove from heat and transfer to a bowl to cool. Set aside.

2. Combine the cucumber, ginger, sugar, 1 tablespoon of the salt, and the vinegar in a bowl. Mix well. Cover and refrigerate for 1 hour.

3. Transfer the cucumber to a square of cheesecloth. Wrap in the cloth and squeeze out and discard the liquid. Transfer the cucumber to a bowl and set aside.

4. Heat the oil in a medium skillet over high heat for 1 to 2 minutes. Add the onion and turmeric powder and sauté until the onion is limp, about 5 minutes. Let cool.

5. Combine the onion, cucumber, the remaining ½ teaspoon salt, and the sesame seeds in a bowl. Toss to mix well, and serve.

Vietnamese Carrot and Daikon Relish

SERVE THIS RELISH with Vietnamese grilled meat and chicken, or use it as a garnish on cool rice vermicelli dishes or as a filling for Vietnamese spring rolls.

1. Combine the sugar, salt, vinegar, fish sauce, and chiles in a saucepan and heat over high heat until the sugar and salt dissolve. Remove from the heat to cool.

2. Combine the grated carrots and daikon in a mixing bowl. Add the sauce and toss lightly. Let sit for 15 minutes before serving. Store the relish in a glass jar with a tight-fitting lid; it will keep for several days in the refrigerator.

Note: If the relish is left to sit for over an hour, it will give off a fair amount of liquid. Do not discard the liquid—use it as a sauce for noodle and grilled dishes. To use the carrot and daikon mixture as a filling for spring rolls, squeeze out the juice.

½ cup sugar
½ teaspoon sea salt
¼ cup rice vinegar
2 tablespoons fish sauce (nam pla)
2 fresh bird chiles or 1 serrano chile, minced
½ cup grated carrots
½ cup grated daikon

Makes 2 cups

Chayote Relish

A FAVORITE SIMPLE RELISH. I eat it by itself as a salad or with a bowl of steamed rice. Or serve it as an accompaniment to a spicy grilled dish such as Otak Otak Nonya-Style Spicy Fish Cakes (page 50). Sumac powder can be bought in Middle Eastern markets.

1 medium chayote, peeled and diced
1 teaspoon crushed red pepper
½ teaspoon sea salt
½ teaspoon paprika
½ teaspoon sumac powder
1 tablespoon fresh lime juice
1 teaspoon olive oil
6 mint leaves, torn and bruised

Makes 1½ cups

Combine the chayote, red pepper, salt, paprika, sumac powder, and lime juice in a bowl. Mix well. Add the oil and mix to combine. Transfer to a serving bowl and garnish with the mint leaves.

Fruit Ambrosia

I AM CERTAIN that this recipe will become part of your repertoire of favorite dishes. Choose seasonal fruits with different textures, and spice them up with the dressing. Serve this salad instead of coleslaw or potato salad with barbecued steak, pork chops, chicken, or hamburger.

1. Dry-roast the coconut in a small skillet over high heat, sliding the skillet back and forth over the burner to prevent burning, until the coconut is golden, 2 to 3 minutes. Remove from the heat and let cool.

2. Combine the lime juice, fish sauce, sugar, salt, and chiles in a bowl. Add the diced fruit, celery, and shallot. Toss gently to mix then add the lime zest. Toss to combine.

3. Transfer to a serving bowl, garnish with the dry-roasted coconut and mint leaves, and serve.

3 tablespoons grated coconut
(see page 135)
2 tablespoons fresh lime juice
1 tablespoon fish sauce (nam pla)
¼ cup sugar
¼ teaspoon sea salt
2 fresh bird chiles or 1 serrano
chile, minced
1 apple, pear, or mango, cored or
seeded and diced
1 cup diced pineapple
1 rib celery, thinly sliced
1 shallot, thinly sliced
Grated zest of 1 lime
6 mint leaves, torn and bruised

Makes 4 servings

Mail-Order Sources

Adriana's Caravan
409 Vanderbilt Street
Brooklyn, NY 11218
800-316-0820
Fax: 718-436-9565
adrianascaravan@aol.com

Midori Mart
2104 Chestnut Street
Philadelphia, PA 19103
215-569-3381
Fax: 215-569-3308
www.midorimart.com

Temple of Thai
P.O. Box 112
Carroll, IA 51401
877-519-0709
712-792-0860
Fax: 712-792-0698
www.templeofthai.com

ThaiGrocer/SEC
3161 North Cambridge Street
Suite 507
Chicago, IL 60657
Tel/Fax: 773-477-6268
www.thaigrocer.com

Thai Grocery
5014 North Broadway Street
Chicago, IL 60640
773-561-5345
Fax: 773-561-5522

Uwajimaya
519 6th Avenue South
Seattle, WA 98104
800-889-1928; 206-624-6248
www.uwajimaya.com
www.asiafood.org

Bibliography

Anderson, Susan. *Indonesian Flavors.* Berkeley, California: Frog Ltd., c/o North Atlantic Books, 1995.

Aung Aung Talk. *Under the Golden Pagoda: The Best of Burmese Cooking.* San Francisco: Chronicle Books, 1993.

The Food of Malaysia. Singapore: Periplus, 1999.

Fu, Pei Mei. *Pei Mei's Chinese Cook Book, Volume I.* Taiwan: Chinese Cooking Institute, 1969.

Lee, Chin Koon. *Mrs. Lee's Cookbook.* Singapore: Eurasia Press, 1976.

Naipinij, Kobkaew. *Aharn Thai.* Thailand: Semadhama Publishing House, 1999.

Noh, Chin-hwa. *Practical Korean Cooking.* Elizabeth, New Jersey: Hollym International Corporation, 1985.

Phai Sing. *Traditional Recipes of Laos.* Totnes, England: Prospect Books, 1995.

Index